PHONICS PATHWAYS

Written and Illustrated by Dolores G. Hiskes

Dorbooks®

To my GREAT FAMILY:
JOHNNY, for his love, support and ideas . . .
(and especially patience!)
ROBIN and GRANT, who inspired a passion for teaching reading
in the very beginning . . .
CHRISTOPHER, for his insights and warm interest . . .
MOM and DAD, eternally . . .
and to all of my WONDERFUL STUDENTS,
who have taught me
so much.

Publisher's Cataloging in Publication
(Prepared by Quality Books Inc.)

Hiskes, Dolores G.
Phonics pathways / written and illustrated by Dolores G. Hiskes.
-- 6th ed.
p. cm.
Audience: K-6th grade.
Preassigned LCCN: 91-067093.
ISBN 0-9620967-6-8

1. Reading (Elementary)--Phonetic method. I. Title.

LB1573.H58 1993 372.4'145
QB193-20088

Dorbooks®
P.O. Box 2588
Livermore, CA 94551, U.S.A.
510-449-6983

REGULAR CLASSROOM (K-5)

"Thank you for allowing me to use your specially-designed phonics system this year in my classroom. I am very certain that my second-grade students have benefited from your material.

"As a classroom teacher, I have found a real need in reading curriculum for good, consistent phonics. Children need a solid, sequential program which builds upon previously learned skills with small, incremental steps toward the whole. Your program offers just the right degree in advances to ensure success. I have found that frustration is almost entirely eliminated with your books.

"From a teacher's perspective, the little proverbs scattered throughout the book offer great insight and encouragement. I have found my students to understand and appreciate them much more than expected.

"I look forward to seeing your logical, well-organized books head the list in reading curriculum!"

--Susan Campbell, Elementary Educator
Livermore, CA

"*Phonics Pathways* is better than apple pie and ice cream! This wonderful book is very easy for students to follow, and is also easy to read with its large, black print. The instructions as you work through the book are equally easy for both parents and teachers to follow. I have had parents with no phonics background at all who are willing and able to help their child by using Mrs. Hiskes' book.

"Children with all learning modes are having success with it because it uses visual, auditory and tactile methods of teaching. About 90% of my kindergarten class are now reading."

--Lynda McCormick, Kindergarten Teacher
Livermore, CA

"I used *Phonics Pathways* as a vital component in my Resource Specialist class serving pre-first through fifth-grade students. I found the book very successful for my primary students, who most quickly learned to blend letters and form words.

"The grandmother of a second-grader wrote that her grandson had 'improved 95% in his reading and understanding of sounds' during the semester he was in resource."

--Carolyn Langfelt, Special Education Teacher
Pleasanton, CA

HOME-SCHOOLING

"*Phonics Pathways* is a complete program. Teaching instruction on each page is brief enough so that no preparation time is needed. Each new concept taught is followed by words, phrases and sentences for practice, so no other reading material is necessary.

"Because of quick movement into blending practice, children are reading three-letter words very soon. Reading practice is designed to improve left-to-right tracking skills, especially important for preventing dyslexic problems.

"*Phonics Pathways* is very reasonably priced for such a complete program."

--Cathy Duffy, Author
Christian Home Educators Curriculum Manual

"We are home-schooling our children, and always know exactly what to do because each page has such clear directions. Lessons are broken down into very small steps, and one skill is built upon another. Ben needed this review to cement these skills concretely in his memory. Two-letter blends were most helpful before trying three-letter words, for example. The whole approach made sense to his logical nature and started him reading."

--Marci Elwess, Home Educator
Antioch, CA

"I never thought I would have to teach my children to read at home. By Christmas our oldest son had been coming home in tears because he couldn't read, and finally we discovered *Phonics Pathways.* In just ten months he developed strong, solid reading skills. Best of all, his five-year-old brother also learned how to read with this book -- now he reads simple books all by himself. It has seemed like a game to him -- it was fun!"

--Tasia W. Florey, Home Economics Teacher
Livermore, CA

LEARNING DISABILITIES

"Your fine book appears to be an excellent tool for both remedial and first-time readers. I especially enjoyed your inclusion of vision therapy exercises and discussion of the necessity for adequate visual skills in the reading process. I appreciate the availability of such a fine resource and will recommend *Phonics Pathways* to patients as needed."

--Amy L. Longacre, O.D.
Foothill Optometric Group, Pleasanton, CA

"When parents ask us what they can use to help their children improve their reading, we recommend *Phonics Pathways*. It is easy to use and engaging for children. The lessons are short and provide a lot of good practice. Children are amused by the whimsical pictures and word usage.

"We find that many children need to learn to track left to right with their eyes. They also need to find patterns and similarities among words. These exercises provide that kind of practice.

"We have used this book with many of our students and can heartily recommend it."

--Joanne Abey, Director
Tutorage Learning Center, Livermore, CA

"As a beginning reading tutor, I was not sure how effective I would be, but I found that your book works almost like magic! I have only to guide and encourage, and the student does all the work because your book makes reading so clear to them. The effort you put into writing *Phonics Pathways* is saving me research time and money, too. I am so grateful to the colleague who recommended your book to me."

--Lindsay Pavel, Reading Tutor
Livermore, CA

"The left-to-right tracking provided by blending sounds together really helps a great deal. I also tutor children with learning disabilities, and it has been successful with 100% of them! One of my tutoring students was chosen by her first-grade teacher as being the most-improved student for the year.

"I really enjoy the fun proverbs in the book -- they feed my spirit, and are uplifting to the child as well.

"This book complements our literature-based program. For me it is the missing link which blends phonics skills with literature-based stories, and is making the best of both programs."

--Lynda McCormick, Tutor
Livermore, CA

OLDER STUDENTS (INCLUDING ADULT) AND ESL

"Here is a brief testimonial, right from the heart. Three of my grandchildren and a twelve-year-old boy are now enthusiastic readers, thanks to you and Dewey. The twelve-year-old had never learned to read and was very frustrated, causing trouble in his fifth-grade class. He is now a confident reader and doing very well in a special class, catching up on the years of schooling he missed. Using *Phonics Pathways* is a joyful learning experience for both teacher and student!"

--Elisabeth Jay, retired Master Reading Teacher
and Tutor, Boise, Idaho

"*Phonics Pathways* has been a powerful, backbone tool at our Adult Literacy tutoring sessions. We needed a basic, simplistic approach due to the extremely low level of my student -- in our program we never know what gaps have occurred in our students' education.

"This book hits the basics in a clear, easy-to-follow style. The large print and uncluttered text are appreciated -- my student doesn't feel intimidated. He especially likes the example words, which 'don't look like the baby ones in my kid's book.' The diacritical marks used throughout the book are especially helpful as my student begins dictionary work, and frequent use of syllables aids in reducing the 'mystery' of multisyllable words. They are increasing his vocabulary in his 'new' language.

"Hooray! My student just dictated his first letter in English -- he's ordered *Phonics Pathways* for himself!"

--Ellen Swartz Pappas, Tutor
Adult Literacy Program, Fremont, CA

"The pleasantest of all diversions

is to sit alone

under a lamp . . .

a book

spread out

before you . . .

and to make friends

with people

of a distant past

you

have

never

known . . ."

..Kenko
1300 AD

INTRODUCTION

READING is a conversation between a reader and an author.
It is our "remote control" to far-away places and long-ago times.
The poem on the previous page, for example, was written over
six hundred years ago! If it were not for the written word,
every time someone dies an entire library would die with them.

WHY PHONICS?

Everyone ought to know the joy of decoding an unfamiliar word, syllable by syllable, exploring the uncharted world of new words and ideas. If we are limited to reading only words we know, and guessing at new words through context clues, we are confined within the boundaries of our current vocabularies and thoughts, interpreting things only from within our own shallow perspectives.

About 44 sounds and 200 letter groups account for the great majority of words in the English language, and can usually be taught successfully by the end of first grade. When children enter first grade, their comprehension vocabulary is estimated to be upward of 20,000 words. Phonics is the clearest connecting link between this vocabulary and the printed page. After learning these sound-to-symbol skills, most children are able to read almost anything their speaking and listening vocabulary, and interest, allows -- unaltered by "readability formulas" or simplified in any other way. They are not limited to reading only words that have been memorized by shape or outline from vocabulary lists.

Phonics should be taught like any other complex skill such as learning how to dance or play the piano. One note or step (or sound) is learned at a time, and very gradually combined into more complicated chords and routines (blends and syllables). Sight-reading whole groups of notes at a time, or smoothly combining steps into an entire dance routine (or reading words and sentences), is what occurs naturally as a result of training and practice, and is never used as a teaching tool to begin with. Simple sub-skills are learned first, then slowly combined into more complicated ones until the subject is completely mastered. Phonics is the *process*, sight reading is the *result*.

Children have different learning modes. But it is misleading to refer to auditory *versus* visual, or phonics *versus* sight. Even with phonics, you still have to *see* the letters and syllables. Even with sight, you still have to *hear* the word you are looking at. A good reading program really should first organize and categorize the English language into the logical patterns that comprise more than 95% of it, and then use a multisensory approach to teach these patterns. Visual, auditory, or kinesthetic children are all able to learn, because of the multisensory approach which addresses each learning style. It will meet the needs of *every* child, correcting and overcoming individual weaknesses whether they be tendencies to reverse and confuse letters when reading, writing or hearing. We shall call this method BASIC PHONICS.

DON'T WE TEACH PHONICS NOW?

Basic phonics is not usually taught today. A variation is sometimes presented in which whole words, usually the names of colors, are taught along with letter sounds. If a student needs assistance, "phonetic hints" may be given by naming the beginning and ending sounds of a word, but students must then guess to fill in the middle part. At other times, sounds may be pulled from the middle of a word if a student needs assistance. The critical, intermediate step of teaching blending and syllabication skills is not usually included. Spelling words are taken from the story being read, in a random fashion. (What if we had to learn math times tables randomly -- 9 x 7, 12 x 8, and 6 x 13? It would be very difficult to learn and remember them!) Since each word is first memorized by its look or shape, the results of this "mixed" approach are not too different from those of whole-word methods. This is the phonics method used in most schools and tutoring institutions today, and the majority of phonics workbooks available in stores also reflect this approach. We shall call it INCIDENTAL PHONICS.

In summary, incidental phonics teaches letter sounds *after* words have already been learned by their configuration -- basic phonics teaches how to *build* words using letter sounds and spelling patterns. The words "blue" and "yellow," for example, are learned along with other words having "ue" and "ow" vowel digraphs in each of these spelling patterns -- the same way we learn math times tables, by pattern. Sight words are not introduced until letter sounds and blending skills are firmly established, and there are fewer of them than is commonly thought.

If basic phonics is so effective, then why is it not used more widely today? Most likely it is because for over 40 years we have not only been without phonics primers, but also textbooks and courses in teachers' colleges that include this kind of instruction. Most of the old basic phonics textbooks have long been out of print.

WHAT TEACHING METHODS DO WE USE TODAY?

LOOK-SAY has been the most widely-used reading program in America for over 40 years. Each word is memorized individually by its configuration or outline. Approximately 500 words per year are taught -- about 1,500 words by the end of third grade. Some experts estimate that by third grade a child's comprehension vocabulary is about 35,000 words. This means that even the students who can learn by this method still are unable to decode over 90% of the words they can understand! That is why look-say readers are severely edited and simplified, incorporating only words children already know how to read.

Newest on the reading scene, the LITERATURE or WHOLE LANGUAGE approach teaches reading by exposing students to good, classic literature instead of the old look-say readers. Proponants say that by replacing what they feel were boring, repetitive primers with colorful, exciting classics children will be motivated to read, and will pick up this skill automatically if they are exposed to all of these wonderful books. The premise is that being able to read is a developmental skill just as being able to walk or talk is, and that children do not need reading or writing taught as separate subjects. They will become fluent readers when they are developmentally ready. If anyone should need special help, sounds are pulled from words as needed -- incidental phonics.

Students are encouraged to guess at words through context clues -- story meaning is stressed over word accuracy. These clues may indeed help students become better guessers, but is guessing at a word really the same thing as reading it? For example, the words "laparoscopy" and "lobotomy" each begin and end with the same letters, and have a similar shape. Both have similar meanings when taken in context. What if a surgeon needed to read one of these words on a patient's chart prior to surgery, and was only able to "read" it by its shape, beginning and ending letters, and context clues? With basic phonics, these words would be read by syllables: "lap-a-ros-co-py" or "lo-bot-o-my." Is there not a world of difference between being *almost* right and *exactly* right? Guessing at a word is *not* the same thing as reading it!

Almost everyone would agree that "reading for meaning" should be a primary objective with any reading method. The question is, how is this goal best achieved? In my experience if a student is able to effortlessly decode his already considerable comprehension vocabulary, he is joyously freed to "read for meaning" instead of having to struggle while "meaning to read." He can focus on the *meaning* of what he is reading because the *mechanics* of sound-to-symbol skills have already been learned and practiced until they are automatic -- just as a concert pianist is able to focus on the *meaning* of the music he is playing, because the individual notes have long ago been learned and practiced until recall was automatic.

WHAT ABOUT DYSLEXIA?

When words are learned as a whole in beginning reading, the eyes are not trained to move from left to right, frequently resulting in letter or word reversals. It has been my experience in over 25 years of tutoring that many students labeled dyslexic no longer reversed letters after having been taught basic phonics. This was puzzling at first, but I soon came to realize how important knowing and blending letter sounds is in the reading process. It is this step which develops the skill of reading smoothly from left to right. Eye muscles are patterned and trained to track smoothly across the page. I began to wonder -- perhaps the students who no longer had dyslexic symptoms after having been taught basic phonics were not really dyslexic to begin with, but were only suffering from a lack in their educational training?

Dyslexia certainly is a difficult and complex problem, and has no easy answers. Perhaps it is of interest to note that specialists frequently treat dyslexia by using exercises and machines to train eyes to track smoothly from left to right. The teaching method used in *Phonics Pathways* has a similar effect -- in this case, eye tracking skills are acquired by blending letter sounds, syllables, words, phrases and finally complete sentences of gradually increasing complexity.

My students who were truly dyslexic needed much more time and practice to build words by syllables and develop fluent blending skills. However, all of them have learned to read well eventually, no matter how serious a problem they may have had to begin with.

It is essential that children who reverse letters or words receive training in blending letter sounds and syllables when learning how to read. The time it takes to acquire these skills will vary greatly with each child, but the end result will be ease and fluency of reading with excellent comprehension -- a genuine and effortless enjoyment of all the wonderful stories in today's literature-based curriculum.

The brain is not unlike a computer insofar as memory and retrieval are concerned. We might think of basic phonics as a software program -- the logical framework into which patterns and categories of words are organized and filed. Words can be more quickly retrieved when reading, and skills do not fade. Learning to read by logical patterns also teaches students to think clearly and sequentially -- a skill which enhances everything children do. Math frequently improves noticeably as reading develops, and spelling improves dramatically.

With whole-word teaching methods such as look-say or literature, words are learned individually, as a whole. Each word is stored in its own "document" in the brain, making retrieval for many students time-consuming and difficult. Progress can remain slow and uncertain. Sometimes the brighter the child the more difficulty he may have, since his logical mind can rebel unless he is able to connect it all into a framework that makes sense. Trying to teach young children how to read using a whole-word method can result in highly stressed, fearful youngsters who feel they are failures when they are unable to learn.

WHEN SHOULD CHILDREN LEARN HOW TO READ?

Children can benefit from early reading and language instruction in pre-school and kindergarten. Four to six-year olds can and should be taught letter sounds and combinations to provide a solid foundation of letter sounds and blending skills. All children this age love to make noises, build things and take them apart. This is the proper age to begin teaching good phonics skills!

Some children will be able to build words faster than others. Others may be able to sound out a word rather quickly, but it may be months before they are able to read even short phrases. It is the ability to put these skills together which allows children to read books. This stage is true "reading readiness," and varies greatly with each child. It is a developmental stage which depends upon how mature his nervous system is, and when his eyes are able to track smoothly from left to right across a page. Outside factors, such as illness or allergies, also affect this readiness. It has nothing to do with intelligence, any more than wearing glasses does.

It is not my experience that reading itself is a developmental skill. While some students do learn how to read without direct reading instruction, many others can not. There are people who learn another language or how to play the piano on their own, but most of us do better with instruction. When we learn another language, we must study the sounds, syllables and structure of that language. Is there really any good reason why learning to read the English language should be any different?

Note: Throughout this book I have used the word "him" when referring to a student. This was done for simplicity, and refers to male and female students equally.

ACKNOWLEDGEMENTS

So many people to thank, and so little space . . . Tom Hanover, John Gordon and Bob Toms for business assistance I couldn't have done without . . . Susan Ebbers for being the first teacher to try my book (and for so many helpful suggestions!) . . . Janet Loughran-Smith for being the first principal to use it (in-school tutoring program) . . . Lindsay for your eagle-eyed proofreading . . . Marci and Ben, for encouraging me and helping to launch my new career . . . . . Tasia for your helpful and well-thought-out feedback . . . Lorraine (all the titles we considered!) . . . Dee, Joel, Sophie and Leslie for your astute insights . . . Mom, Marge, other family and friends, and all the original authors from all over the world (whoever they are and whereever they now may be) for so many great proverbs . . . Johnny for never minding the 5:00 a.m. "put-put-put" of the computer . . . and last but not least Kiwi, who faithfully positioned herself on the printer beside me, purring and proofing the entire time . . .
so many others, and no more room . . .
. . . but you know who you are . . .
. . . and I thank you, one and all!

OTHER PUBLICATIONS

Coming soon:

My Little Short-Vowel Dictionary. A pocketbook reference containing only vowels, one per page, with multiple pictures illustrating each short sound. Teaches and reinforces short-vowel sounds.

The Short-Vowel Shuffle. A card game consisting of three sets of vowels and wild "eyes" cards. Reinforces short-vowel sounds (no pictures) in an amusing and enjoyable fashion.

My Blue Book of Blends. A small, kid-sized book which teaches and reinforces blending and syllabication skills. (Presupposes knowledge of short-vowel sounds and consonants.)

The Train Game. A set of "train-car" cards including vowels, consonants, digraphs, various endings, and syllables. Patterns eyes to track smoothly from left to right by teaching graduated blending and syllabication skills. (Presupposes knowledge of short-vowel sounds and consonants.)

. . . and more . . .

ABOUT PHONICS PATHWAYS

Phonics Pathways is a complete reading manual for beginning and remedial readers of all ages. The sounds and spelling patterns of the English language are slowly built and recombined into syllables, words, phrases, and finally sentences of gradually increasing complexity. Each new step utilizes skills previously learned for continuous review and reinforcement.

Single, short-vowel sounds are presented first -- this knowledge is the basic foundation necessary for building good reading and spelling skills. Only one sound is learned at a time. (Can you not remember names more easily when you meet people one at a time, rather than in an entire group at once?)

Two-letter blends are introduced next, reviewing all short-vowel sounds with each new consonant learned. This important but often overlooked step is difficult for many children, and takes time. It teaches children to blend sounds together smoothly, and trains their eyes to track from left to right. It is this step which begins to correct and overcome any tendency to reverse or confuse letters.

Three-letter words are then built, followed by slowly increasing combinations -- consonant blends, digraphs, dipthongs, etc. Words are first read alone, then in two-word phrases, and gradually combined to make longer phrases and sentences. This continues and expands upon the eye training mentioned above, progressively strengthening the ability of eye muscles to move together smoothly from left to right across a page. This kind of training is similar to eye exercises specialists frequently use when treating dyslexia, but is incorporated within the lessons themselves. All children are able to learn easily, and dyslexics benefit most dramatically!

These sounds and syllables are integrated into meaningful words as soon as possible with each lesson, beginning with three-letter words. They are not taught first as a separate set of disconnected skills to memorize before being applied. Blending sounds into words as you learn them gives meaning to them, and makes them much easier to remember. Memory experts have long known how important this principle is.

Phonics Pathways uses a multisensory approach, adjusting to all learning styles whether audio, visual, or kinesthetic. Every letter introduced is seen, heard, traced, spoken and written. Each letter is lavishly illustrated with multiple pictures beginning with this sound, producing an effortless fusion of letter and sound in the child's memory. Several pictures more accurately illustrate the subtle range of sounds comprising each short-vowel sound, similar in effect to a 3-D hologram. Visually-oriented children and bilingual students who can speak English but not read it benefit especially from this approach.

There is no guessing. Trying to understand the general meaning of a text through context clues is not the same thing as being able to read it accurately. *All* persons need to be able to read with precision, whether filling out an application form, charting a flight pattern, or looking over a patient's records prior to surgery! The ability to read accurately is taught from the very first lesson.

There are no choices to make. Even considering a wrong answer makes an imprint on the brain, which then takes more time and energy to unlearn. (If a music teacher taught you how to play the piano by having you choose which note was correct from a list, just think of how it would slow you down!)

Large, 24-point letters are used for the lessons. Even with proper glasses students often struggle with smaller letters when first learning, and find it much simpler to learn from larger letters. Once reading is established, it's easier to read finer print.

Both styles of "a" and "g" are presented -- we read them one way, but write them another. This is a difficult concept for many beginning readers, but we do need to know them both.

Clear, simple directions begin each lesson, and tell you exactly what to do and how to do it. Parents as well as professionals are able to use this book easily and effectively -- no prep time or prior knowledge of phonics is needed. Frequent checkpoints tell you when and how to review, and when to proceed. This flexible approach carefully monitors progress and determines pace, adjusting easily to fast or slow learners of any age or attention span.

The diacritical marks used are consistent with those found in commonly used dictionaries. No sight words are introduced until well after basic phonics skills are firmly established. Younger children enjoy Dewey the Bookworm as he guides them through these lessons, and older students appreciate the proverbs sprinkled throughout the book, encouraging values such as hard work, patience, personal integrity and self-confidence.

Phonics Pathways is an ideal complement to today's literature-based reading programs. It provides the tools and teaches the skills needed to unlock and decode all of these wonderful old stories. Working about ten to thirty minutes a day, most students are able to read this classic literature within a year.

William Blake once said:

> "There are things that are known
> and things that are unknown --
> in between are only doors."

Phonics Pathways is the key that will open the door of literacy for *everyone!*

. . . And remember, KEEP ON TRYING . . .
it's often the LAST KEY in the BUNCH
that OPENS the LOCK!!!

CONTENTS

1--BASICS
Short-vowel sounds ... 1
Consonants and two-letter blends (cv) ... 7
Three-letter words (cvc) ... 27
"K-c-ck" ... 36

2--INTRODUCTION TO ENDINGS (SHORT-VOWEL WORDS)
Double-consonnt endings ... 40
"Y" ending ... 49
Twin-consonant endings ... 53

3--CONSONANT DIGRAPH ENDINGS ... 54
"Sh" ending ... 55
"Th" ending ... 56
"Ch-tch" ending ... 58
"Ng" endings ("-ing, -ang, -ung, -ong") ... 60
"Nk" endings ("-ink, -ank, -unk") ... 64

4--SIMPLE LONG-VOWEL SOUNDS ... 67

5--ADDING ENDINGS (SHORT AND LONG-VOWEL WORDS)
"-Y, -ing, -ed, -er" ... 83

6--MULTI-SYLLABLE WORDS ... 88

7--PLURAL, POSSESSIVE, AND "X" ... 90

8--CONSONANT DIGRAPH BEGINNINGS ... 93
"Sh-, th-, ch-, wh-, qu-"

9--DOUBLE-CONSONANT BEGINNINGS ... 103
"Bl-, fl-, pl-, cl-, gl-, sl-"

10--PALINDROMES ... 107

11--DOUBLE-CONSONANT BEGINNINGS
"Sm-, sn-, st-, sp-, sc-sk-" ... 108
"Br-, cr-, dr-, fr-, gr-, pr-, tr-" ... 112

12--"R" MODIFIED VOWELS
"Är = ar" ... 116
"Ôr = or, ore, our, oar" ... 117
"Ur = er, ir, ur, or, ear" ... 120

13--LONG-VOWEL DIGRAPHS ... 125
"Ā = ai, ay" ... 126
"Ē = ie" ("ee, ea" learned earlier) ... 129
"Ī = ie, y" ... 131
"Ō = oa, oe, ow" ... 133
"Ū (oo) = oo, ew, ue, ui, ou" ... 135

14--"C = S" ("Ce, ci, cy") 138
"Ē = ei after c" digraph 139

15--VOWEL DIPTHONGS
"Oi = oi, oy" 141
"Ou = ou, ow" 143

16--"GE, GI, DGE = J" 146

17--MORE ENDINGS
"Y = -ies, etc." 149
"F = -ves" 150

18--NEW VOWEL DIGRAPH SOUNDS
"Ŏo = oo" (also "ould, u") 152
"Ô = aw, au" (also "al, all, o") 155

19--THREE-LETTER CONSONANT BEGINNINGS 159

20--SHORT-VOWEL SPELLING PATTERNS
"Ĕ = ea, ai" 161
"Ĭ = y" 162
"Ŭ = o, ou, oo, a" 164
"Ŭ = ə " 165

21--CONTRACTIONS 167

22--SILENT LETTERS
"-le" 169
"K, w, l, b, t, h" 171
"Gh" ("ī = igh" and "ô = ough, augh") 174

23--LONG "A" SPELLING PATTERNS 177
"Ā = ei, eigh, ey, ea"

24--"SE = Z," "PH, GH = F," AND "CH = K" 180

25--ANOTHER "R" MODIFIED VOWEL SOUND 185
"Âr = -air, -are, -ear, -ere"

26--A SPELLING GRAB BAG
Homonyms and Homophones 187
Homographs 188
Multi-syllable word endings (short vowels) 189
"-Ce" and "-ge" plus endings 190
"-Able" or "-ible" 190

27--PREFIXES 191
"Pre-, sub-, re-, auto-, un-, dis-, inter-, super-"

28--SUFFIXES 194
"-Tion, -sion, -able, -ness, -ful, -less, -ment"

29--COMPOUND WORDS 197

30--"BUILDING BLOCKS" 198

HELPFUL HINTS

Try to be gently persistent in setting aside just a few minutes a day for this book at first, but do not hurry or pressure your student. It is the habit of sitting down together for a lesson that is important to establish -- after awhile, you will gradually find yourselves spending more time with these lessons. Working just ten minutes a day can result in real progress. Find a time and place that is quiet and satisfactory for both of you. Go slowly, and genuinely praise his efforts. There may even be times when it's best to put this book aside for awhile. Many things affect a child's receptiveness to learning, such as maturity, attention span, health, hyperactivity, etc. These vary greatly with each child, and even from day to day with the same child.

Find out the things he enjoys and is good at, and talk about them! Tell him everyone needs help with something, and that many famous people had a lot of trouble learning how to read and write. If he is a remedial student, discuss how it's much more difficult to unlearn something and then re-learn it the correct way -- use imagery in creative ways. For example, if a store is only one mile away but he walks a mile in the wrong direction, he must first turn around and retrace his steps back to where he started, and then walk another mile to the store. He has walked three miles in all -- *three times* the distance that it would have taken if he had gone the correct way to *begin* with! It's the same thing with time and energy spent when re-learning how to read. Realizing this will help him be a little more patient with himself.

Children who are read to usually show a greater desire to read themselves. Find a good book from the library or bookstore, and read to him after each lesson, as a special treat. There are excellent guides available for books suitable for each age level; your librarian can help as well. Think of things to reward him with -- coins, stickers, etc. Give him one after each lesson to put in a small jar (or booklet.) Do not let him keep this until some agreed-upon time (when it's full, end of year, birthday, etc.) but let him hold it after each lesson while you are reading to him, so that he can count his money (or stickers). Remind him that each coin (or sticker) represents a lesson he has had, and his skills are growing along with his collection. Students love hearing this! Consider getting a book of jokes or riddles, and read one to him at the end of each lesson. Play "memory" with him to improve his concentration and memory. Find a box with a cover, and let him help you collect things to put into it, such as a pin, ball, eraser, envelope, bottle, paper clip, nut, sock, etc. Have him put one item at a time in the box, cover it, and then tell you what is inside. It's a lot of fun, and really helps expand his ability to concentrate and remember sequentially. These times together should be enjoyable and fun for both of you!

Is your child clumsy, tired a lot, impulsive, and/or hyperactive? Does he have poor coordination and/or a short attention span? These children frequently have learning problems. Among the many causes for these symptoms may be allergies and sensitivities, which some allergists feel can take a systemic form instead of a more common, localized form such as hay fever. Experts disagree that this can be a factor. But you might consider asking your doctor for a safe elimination diet to try, and see if it makes a difference. At least you can try to avoid junk foods, or those with a lot of chemical additives. It makes a real difference with many children.

Get his eyes checked -- he could have a vision problem. Some experts feel that not only might a child need glasses, but if he is clumsy and has poor coordination he might also benefit from vision training -- exercises designed to help eyes move together and improve eye-hand-motor coordination skills. The premise is that developing these skills is very helpful to the reading process. Experts disagree, but in my experience it has been most beneficial to many students. The last two pages of the book contain some of the best exercises frequently used in this type of training. Good luck. . . have fun . . . and remember to take just *one small step at a time!!!*

. . . and now . . .

". . . . . . Whatever

you

CAN

do . . .

. . . or DREAM

you

can . . . . .

BEGIN IT!!!"

--Goethe

BASICS: SHORT-VOWEL SOUNDS

We shall begin by learning the SHORT SOUND of the FIVE VOWELS in the English Language. We shall learn them one at a time -- there is one vowel per page. Try to spend just a few minutes, once or twice a day, learning these vowel sounds.

1. Listen carefully to the NAME and BEGINNING SOUND of each picture on the page. Especially notice the beginning sound:

   "Atom, 'a,' ant, 'a,' apple, 'a,' A, 'a.' Is it the SAME sound or is it DIFFERENT? It is the SAME SOUND. THIS is the short sound of the letter 'a.'"

2. Listen to these words once more, but this time YOU say each beginning sound. After that, say both the name AND beginning sound of each picture.

3. Next, say the name and short sound of the letter "a," and TRACE each letter with your fingertip. SPECIAL NOTE: Make SURE you start at the correct place and move your finger in the correct direction when you trace these letters. There are many little workbooks available showing you how to do this, as well as the inside cover of some writing pads. If problems persist in this area, try making (or buying) large sandpaper letters to trace -- it's helpful!

4. WRITE the letter, and say this short sound again. Remember to first trace the sandpaper letter with your finger if you are having difficulty forming these letters in the correct way. (If you cannot write, just listen to this sound and point. Substitute pointing for writing throughout this manual.)

5. Read the REVIEW WINDOWBOX at the bottom, then write it from dictation.

6. Repeat these instructions with each of the four remaining vowels.

And now let us meet DEWEY,* a truly wise "bookworm" who will be your personal guide throughout this book. He adds his special thoughts and inspiration to encourage you along the way.

Have you ever gone into a roomful of people and been introduced to MANY PEOPLE at ONE TIME? Think of how HARD it was to try and remember all of their names! Perhaps you couldn't. But if you met them just ONE AT A TIME, you would have NO PROBLEM.

It's the SAME THING with learning how to read, or learning how to do ANYTHING, for that matter.

Just ONE SMALL STEP AT A TIME will DO it!

*Dewey D. System, Bookwormus Giganticus
© 1982 Dolores G. Hiskes

Ăă Ăɑ̆

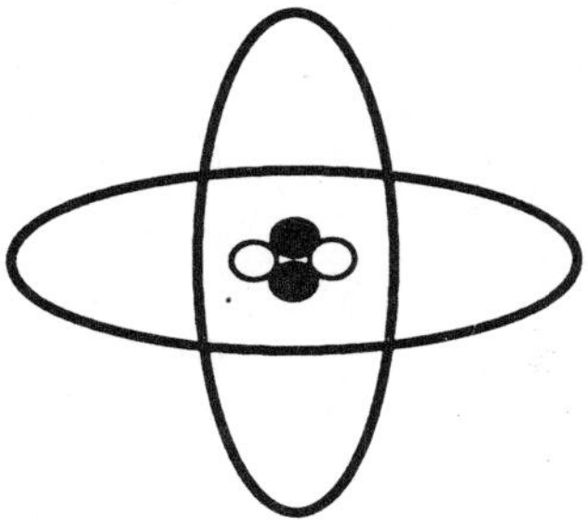

There are TWO WAYS of writing "a."

Here is how we READ it: "a"

And here is how we WRITE it: "ɑ"

We need to know them BOTH!

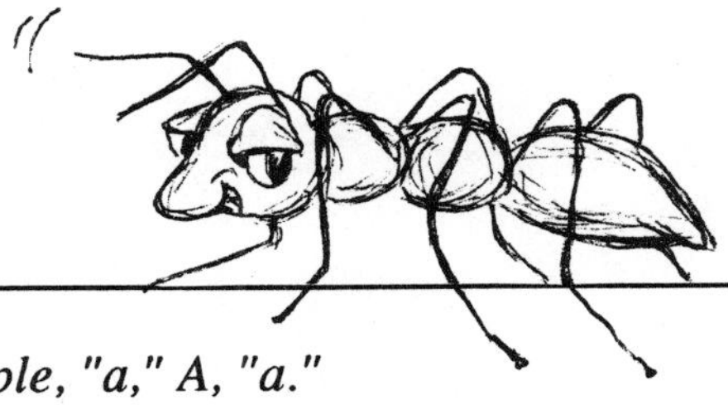

Atom, "a," ant, "a," apple, "a," A, "a."

The little mark you see above these letters is called a DIACRITICAL mark. There are DIFFERENT MARKS for DIFFERENT SOUNDS.

These marks tell you EXACTLY how to pronounce letters and syllables. They are the KEY that shows you how to SOUND OUT a word when you look it up in the dictionary.

Knowing this code is VERY HANDY!!!

a ɑ

Ĕĕ

If it's HARD for you to write these lessons from dictation, try saying the sound again YOURSELF, after hearing it. It may help. (You can even peek at it if you need to!)

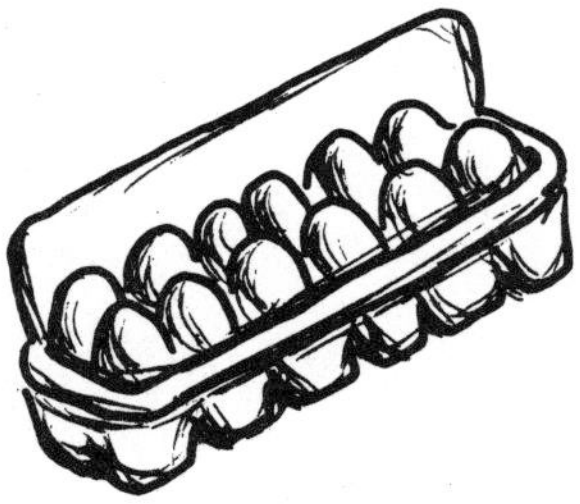

Eggs, "e," evergreen, "e," exercise, "e," E, "e."

Educators such as Maria Montessori have LONG KNOWN that when we use ALL of our senses to learn something, not only is it EASIER TO LEARN, but we DON'T tend to FORGET! That is why we SEE, HEAR, SAY, FEEL, and WRITE each letter we are learning. This is called a MULTI-SENSORY approach to learning, and it makes things SO MUCH EASIER.

It's really AMAZING, when you stop to THINK about it!

a e ɑ

Ĭi

It's REALLY DIFFICULT to tell these sounds apart at first.
Here's a NEAT TRICK that many people find very helpful (as well as fun!):

Let's suppose that you are having trouble being able to tell "i" from "e."
Try saying the "e" pictures using the "i" sound: "iggs, ixercise, ivergreen."
Now say the "i" pictures with the "e" sound: "etch, egloo." See what I mean?

This little ~~ixercise~~ exercise is helpful because when you listen to both the WRONG and RIGHT way of saying these sounds within a word, it is MUCH EASIER to hear the difference between them!

Itch, "i," igloo, "i," I, "i."

The HIGHEST MOUNTAIN
in the WHOLE WORLD
is STILL climbed
by taking only
ONE SMALL STEP AT A TIME...

Just as WE are learning to READ
by taking only
ONE SMALL STEP AT A TIME!!!

a e i ɑ

Ŏŏ

It's MUCH easier to look at these short-vowel sounds JUST for a MINUTE, several times a day, than it is to have LONG STUDY periods. After all, did YOU have to STUDY HARD to learn YOUR OWN NAME? Of course not! You learned it EASILY because you heard someone SAY it to you, off and on, each day since your birth.

Write these vowels in large letters on cards, as you learn them, and put them where you will see them a lot. Take a look at them every so often, and say them out loud. You will be SURPRISED at how QUICKLY you will learn them!

Octopus, "o," ostrich, "o," O, "o."

The GREATEST BOOK in the WHOLE WORLD begins with JUST ONE WORD . . .

. . . and THAT word begins with only ONE LETTER.

So did WE begin with only one letter.
Easy does it -- SLOW but SURE . . . we'll take just
ONE SMALL STEP AT A TIME!!!

a e i o ɑ

Ŭŭ

Ugly, "u," umbrella, "u," U, "u."

And THAT ENDS THE VOWELS!

On the next page is your first review.
Please remember ONE THING when reviewing:
D O N ' T   E V E R   G U E S S ! ! !
A wrong answer leaves an imprint on your brain, which then takes MORE time and energy to UNlearn.

ALWAYS look back at the letter pictures until you know these sounds well enough NOT to. It makes things so much easier -- and in the LONG run, you will learn FASTER.

a e i o u

SHORT-VOWEL REVIEW

Aa	Ee	Ii	Oo	Uu
a	i	e	ɑ	o
u	a	o	e	i
i	u	ɑ	a	e
o	e	a	i	u

Review this page once a day, until you are able to read, write and say each sound EASILY.

Have someone PANTOMIME a word for any sound you may forget -- such as bite an apple ("a"), lift an arm up and down ("e" exercise), scratch ("i" itch), wave arms around ("o" octopus), or make an ugly face ("u").

DO look back at the letter pictures as OFTEN as you NEED to . . . but D O N O T P R O C E E D until you are able to read these sounds WITHOUT looking at the pictures.

Knowing these short-vowel sounds will REALLY HELP your SPELLING, as well as your reading!

CONSONANTS AND TWO-LETTER BLENDS

Now we shall learn some CONSONANTS, and combine them with vowels to make TWO-LETTER BLENDS. (A consonant is any letter that is not a vowel.) Seventeen consonants will be introduced for this exercise, one per page.

This knowledge will eventually enable you to sound out even the LONGEST of words, syllable by syllable -- without guessing. What are SYLLABLES? Why, syllables are all of the small parts that a word can be broken into -- they are nothing but (mostly) two and three-letter blends! We build bricks to make a house, and we build syllables to make words.

Learning to blend sounds together is learning a NEW SKILL. It may not be EASY, at first, but it is very important. It is THIS step which will train your eye muscles to "track" smoothly across the page from left to right, and allow you to actually read whole sentences, and eventually books. We shall begin with two-letter blends in this section, and slowly add more sounds and syllables later, as we work through this book.

Take whatever time you need to go through this section, until you are able to blend these sounds easily and effortlessly. It will make subsequent learning SO much faster -- and more fun, as well!

Learning how to read is the same as learning ANY OTHER skill. Take skating, for example. You must first spend a LONG TIME strengthening your muscles, learning balance, and trying simple routines. If you proceed TOO FAST, you could HURT yourself. Perhaps BADLY. But we have ALL seen how experts seem almost to FLY at times, after they have learned their basics. What FUN they seem to be having, and how EASY it all seems! But you can be sure it WASN'T EASY at first -- or perhaps even FUN.

It is the SAME THING with LEARNING HOW TO READ. By adding only ONE LETTER at a TIME, you are training and strengthening your eyes to "track" -- that is, to smoothly read sounds from left to right, slowly building these sounds into words and sentences. This is the SOLID FOUNDATION of READING SKILLS that will allow you to read ANYTHING YOU WANT to read.

How WONDERFUL it will be to be able to "FLY" with BOOKS!

1. NAME each picture on the page, and LISTEN for its BEGINNING SOUND. Each picture begins with the sound of the consonant introduced on that page. (These words also may contain many sounds you have not had yet, such as long-vowel sounds, but you are ONLY to listen for the BEGINNING SOUND of each one.)

2. Now BLEND the consonant sound with the vowel sound. Begin at the top of the ladder, and read the short "a"; then read the two sounds individually as you go across, "s-a"; and NOW blend the sounds together SMOOTHLY, to say "sa". Continue in this manner, moving down the ladder to each vowel as you go.

   ALWAYS look back at the pictures if you are NOT SURE.

3. Read the blends in the review window at the bottom.

4. Write these sounds as you listen to them from dictation. (As mentioned earlier, if you find it too hard to hear these sounds from dictation alone, then say them yourself first. If it is STILL too hard, then you may also take a look at them.)

6. Repeat these instructions with the rest of the consonants in this section.

Try to complete at least one page a day. If any particular consonant blend seems especially difficult to do, repeat it for the next day's lesson.

We review EACH STEP a LOT because we need to know this material at a DEEP LEVEL, almost as well as our OWN NAME. We have to be able to read it AUTOMATICALLY, without having to THINK about it too much.

It's like learning how to ride a bicycle, or drive a car. At FIRST, we need to go SLOWLY and THINK about EVERY STEP INVOLVED.

We would NEVER THINK of going out on a BUSY FREEWAY or down a STEEP HILL our first time out. That comes LATER, when our skills are practiced enough to be AUTOMATIC. THEN it's F U N !!

Ss

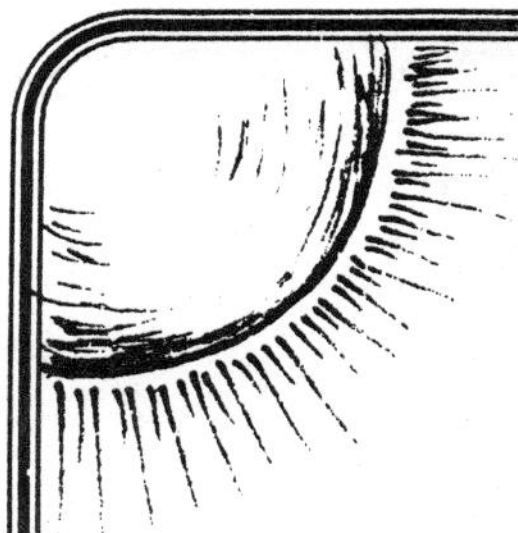

a	s-a	sa
e	s-e	se
i	s-i	si
o	s-o	so
u	s-u	su

You don't have to be GOOD to START, but you have to START to be GOOD!!!

su so si se sa

Sun, star, snake.

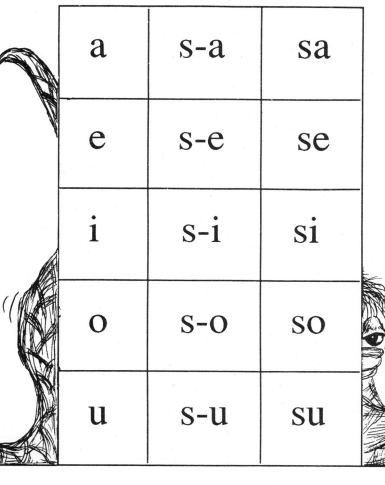

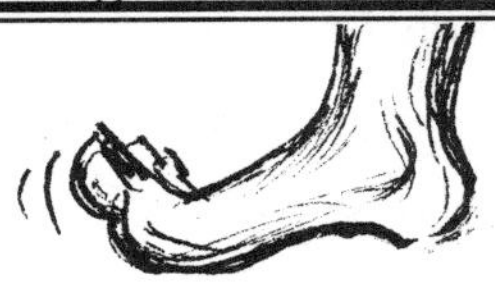

Ff

a	f-a	fa
e	f-e	fe
i	f-i	fi
o	f-o	fo
u	f-u	fu

When READING these blends it is SOMETIMES fun to say REAL WORDS that BEGIN with these blends as you go along -- such as "'fu' as in fun, 'fo' as in fox, 'fi' as in fist, 'fe' as in fetch, 'fa' as in fast," etc.

TRY it, you may LIKE it! The IMPORTANT thing, of course, is to READ THESE BLENDS, whether you add words or not.

fu fo fi fe fa

su se so si

Fish, foot, frog

Rr

a	r-a	ra
e	r-e	re
i	r-i	ri
o	r-o	ro
u	r-u	ru

ru ro ri re ra

fa fe su si

Rain, ring, rabbit

Hh

a	h-a	ha
e	h-e	he
i	h-i	hi
o	h-o	ho
u	h-u	hu

hu ho hi he ha

ra fe si ru

Heart, hammer, hat

Mm

a	m-a	ma
e	m-e	me
i	m-i	mi
o	m-o	mo
u	m-u	mu

A GOOD PLACE to find a HELPING HAND is at the END of your ARM!

mu mo mi me ma

se fa ru hi

Mouse, moon, mushroom

Nn

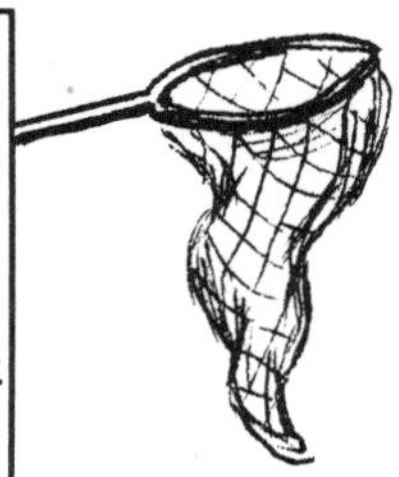

a	n-a	na
e	n-e	ne
i	n-i	ni
o	n-o	no
u	n-u	nu

nu no ni ne na

hu ri fa se

Note, net, nest

Dd

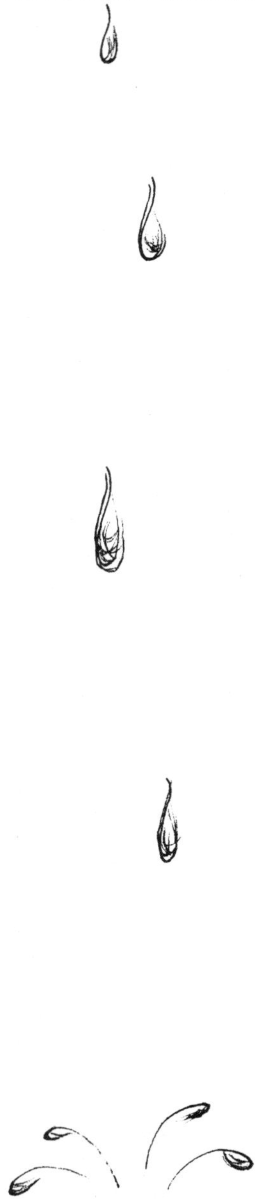

a	d-a	da
e	d-e	de
i	d-i	di
o	d-o	do
u	d-u	du

It's NICE to be IMPORTANT . . . But it's MORE important to be N I C E !!!

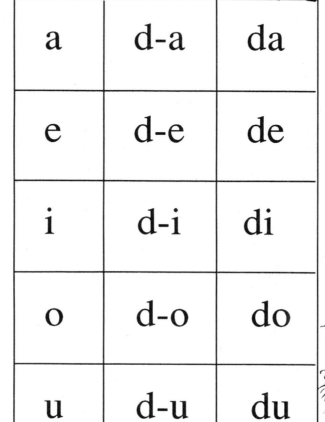

du do di de da

ne mi ho su

da Da-n Dan

Drops, duck, dress

Bb

It's MUCH BETTER to spend just a FEW MINUTES twice a day with this book, rather than studying LONGER, but only several times a WEEK.

Think of brushing your teeth. Would they look ANY BETTER if you brushed them only TWICE A WEEK, but did it for a WHOLE HALF HOUR?

I'll bet they wouldn't even look as NICE!

a	b-a	ba
e	b-e	be
i	b-i	bi
o	b-o	bo
u	b-u	bu

bu bo bi be ba

da ne mi hu

ba ba-n ban

Boy, bee, broom

Tt

a	t-a	ta
e	t-e	te
i	t-i	ti
o	t-o	to
u	t-u	tu

tu to ti te ta

bi da nu mo

ta ta-n tan

Teapot, turtle, tree

Pp

There are
TWO WAYS
to get to the top
of an oak tree.
One is to
sit on an acorn
and WAIT.
The other
is to
CLIMB IT!!!

a	p-a	pa
e	p-e	pe
i	p-i	pi
o	p-o	po
u	p-u	pu

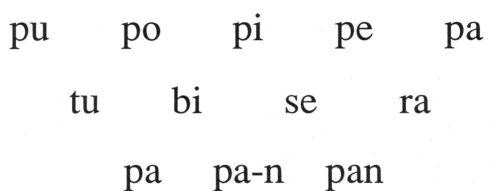

pu po pi pe pa

tu bi se ra

pa pa-n pan

Pumpkin, picture, present

Gg Gg

There are TWO WAYS to write the letter "g."

We READ it THIS way:

"g"

and we WRITE it THIS way:

"g"

a	g-a	ga
e	g-e	ge
i	g-i	gi
o	g-o	go
u	g-u	gu

gu go gi ge ga

gu go gi ge ga

ga ga-s gas

Girl, grapes, gorilla

Jj

a	j-a	ja
e	j-e	je
i	j-i	ji
o	j-o	jo
u	j-u	ju

The BEST ANGLE from which to approach ANY problem is the "TRY-ANGLE"!!!

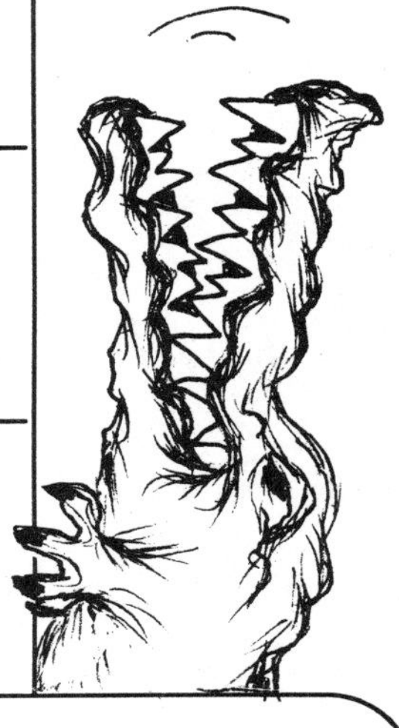

ju jo ji je ja

ge pu gi da

ja ja-m jam

Jacket, juggle, jaws

Ll

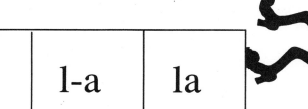

a	l-a	la
e	l-e	le
i	l-i	li
o	l-o	lo
u	l-u	lu

Just take ONE LITTLE STEP at a TIME . . . and then ANOTHER, and then ANOTHER, and ANOTHER, AND ANOTHER, AND ANOTHER, AND ANOTHER, and another, and . . .

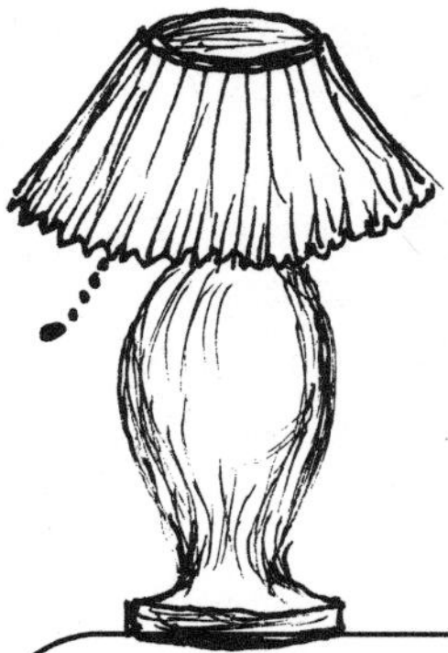

lu lo li le la

ji gu ba te

la la-p lap

Lips, lamp, legs

Vv

a	v-a	va
e	v-e	ve
i	v-i	vi
o	v-o	vo
u	v-u	vu

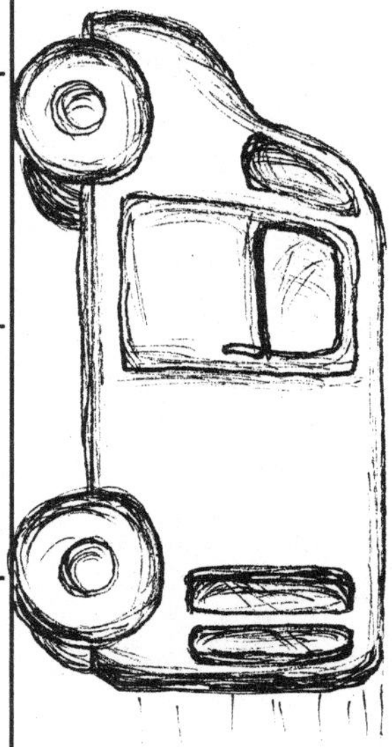

vu vo vi ve va

li fa je go

va va-n van

Van, vegetables

Ww

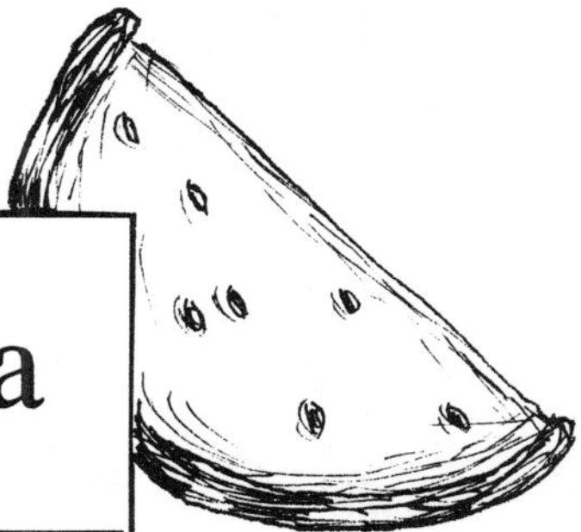

a	w-a	wa
e	w-e	we
i	w-i	wi
o	w-o	wo
u	w-u	wu

You will never get "A-HEAD" of anyone as long as you are trying to get EVEN with them!

wu wo wi we wa

ga te bo su

wa wa-g wag

Wig, wag, watermelon

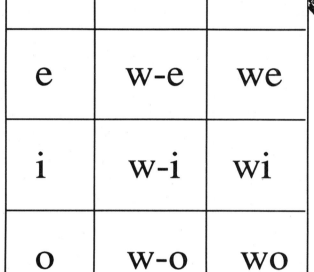

Yy

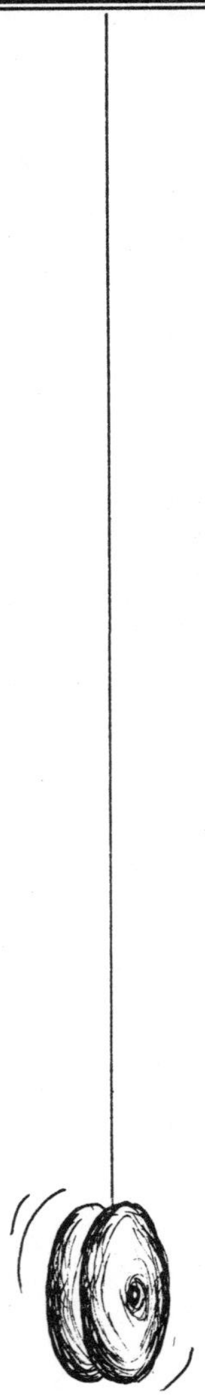

a	y-a	ya
e	y-e	ye
i	y-i	yi
o	y-o	yo
u	y-u	yu

The BEST thing to do behind a person's back is to PAT IT!

yu yo yi ye ya

wi pa gu de

ya ya-p yap

Yo-yo, "yak"

Zz

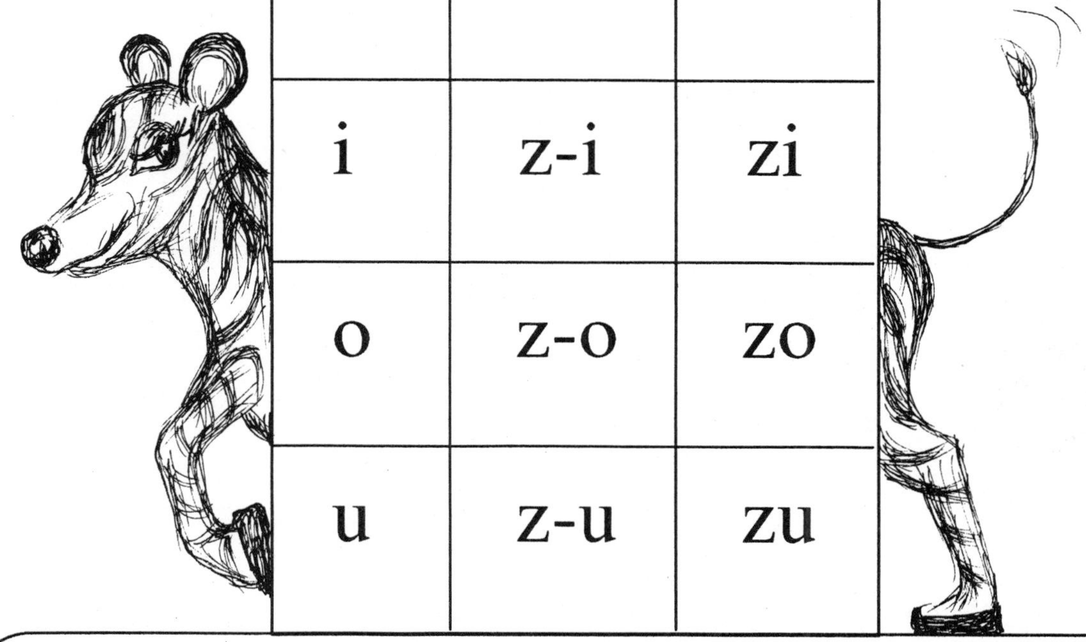

a	z-a	za
e	z-e	ze
i	z-i	zi
o	z-o	zo
u	z-u	zu

zu zo zi ze za

gi va su pe

za za-p zap

Zebra

TWO-LETTER BLEND REVIEW

se	si	fa	fo	he
mu	ye	na	mi	du
ni	ba	tu	pe	gi
je	lu	we	va	zi
so	wi	fe	vu	za

Review this page once a day -- READ these blends, and then WRITE them.

(Those of you who have trouble HEARING these sounds by just reading them SILENTLY may prefer saying them OUT LOUD FIRST, before writing them down. Do this throughout the book for as long as you need to.)

Look back at the letter pictures as much as you need to in order NOT to GUESS, but to THINK it THROUGH.

Take all the time you need, until you are able to read these blends EASILY, WITHOUT peeking back at the pictures.

THREE-LETTER WORDS

Now we shall add a consonant to the end of these two-letter blends, and make three-letter words.

1. Read the two-letter blend out loud, blending the sounds together: "sa."

2. Read this blended sound AGAIN, and now add the sound of the LAST letter: "sa-t."

3. Read the whole word, blending all sounds together SMOOTHLY. Make sure you do not sound out each letter by itself, first. For example, do not say "s-a" or "s-a-t." Read the two-letter blend "sa" first, and THEN add the last letter: "sa-t, sat."

4. Now listen to these words, and then write them from dictation.

5. Read the words in the bottom review window, then write them from dictation.

Try to complete one page a day, and repeat this page for the next day's lesson if needed. It is learning to blend these sounds easily that will get you reading!

Proceed in this manner to the end of this section. Take all the time you need in order to read these words WITHOUT having to sound out each letter first. The time this takes will vary -- it depends upon how soon your eye muscles are strong enough to "track" across a word. It does NOT depend upon how SMART you are! For example, if someone needs to wear glasses, does it mean they are more or less intelligent than someone who does NOT wear glasses?

SPECIAL NOTE TO REMEDIAL STUDENTS: At first, you may find that you need a little more time to complete these lessons than someone who is just learning how to read for the first time. This is perfectly NATURAL, and is to be EXPECTED. You are unlearning ineffective reading methods in order to learn how to read by "building words." Any time we must UNLEARN something in order to learn it correctly, it will always take MORE time and energy than if we had simply learned it correctly in the first place. So . . . please be *P A T I E N T* with yourselves!

Do you know the definition of PATIENCE?
PATIENCE is being able to
IDLE YOUR MOTOR
when you REALLY feel like
S T R I P P I N G Y O U R G E A R S !!!

Read all of the blends first, even if you ARE able to read each word WITHOUT doing this. Why? Because it is GOOD TRAINING for your EYES to practice "tracking" from left to right. Reading will be MUCH EASIER for you. It is like AEROBICS for your EYES. In fact, let's CALL it "EYE-ROBICS" from now on, because that's EXACTLY what it IS! EXERCISE for your EYES! (Please read down one letter group at a time -- "s" words first, etc.)

Ss

sa	sa-d	sad
se	se-t	set
si	si-t	sit
so	so-b	sob
su	su-n	sun

Ff

fa	fa-d	fad
fe	fe-d	fed
fi	fi-n	fin
fo	fo-p	fop
fu	fu-n	fun

Rr

ra	ra-p	rap
re	re-d	red
ro	ro-t	rot
ru	ru-g	rug

Hh

ha	ha-t	hat
he	he-n	hen
ho	ho-t	hot
hu	hu-g	hug

sun fun

red hat

Mm

ma	ma-n	man
me	me-t	met
mi	mi-d	mid
mo	mo-p	mop
mu	mu-g	mug

Nn

na	na-g	nag
ne	ne-t	net
ni	ni-p	nip
no	no-d	nod
nu	nu-t	nut

Dd

da	da-d	dad
de	de-n	den
di	di-g	dig
do	do-t	dot
du	du-d	dud

Bb

ba	ba-d	bad
be	be-t	bet
bi	bi-g	big
bo	bo-p	bop
bu	bu-n	bun

big mug

dig nut

Tt

ta	ta-p	tap
te	te-n	ten
ti	ti-n	tin
to	to-p	top
tu	tu-g	tug

Pp

pa	pa-n	pan
pe	pe-n	pen
pi	pi-n	pin
po	po-t	pot
pu	pu-n	pun

Gg

ga	ga-g	gag
ge	ge-t	get
gi	gi-g	gig
go	go-t	got
gu	gu-m	gum

Jj

ja	ja-m	jam
je	je-t	jet
Ji	Ji-m	Jim
jo	jo-g	jog
ju	ju-g	jug

jam pot

top jet

Ll

la	la-p	lap
le	le-g	leg
li	li-p	lip
lo	lo-b	lob
lu	lu-g	lug

Vv

va	va-n	van
ve	ve-t	vet
vi	vi-m	vim

A HUG is the PERFECT GIFT. . .
. . . one size fits ALL,
and nobody MINDS
if you give it BACK!!

Ww

wa	wa-g	wag
we	we-t	wet
wi	wi-n	win

Yy

ya	ya-m	yam
ye	ye-t	yet
yi	yi-p	yip

lug yam

win van

Aa

da	da-d	dad
na	na-g	nag
sa	sa-p	sap
ra	ra-n	ran
ma	ma-d	mad

Ee

pe	pe-p	pep
pe	pe-n	pen
te	te-n	ten
ge	ge-t	get
ne	ne-t	net

JUMPING TO CONCLUSIONS
is not HALF as good exercise
as DIGGING FOR FACTS!!!

Ii

si	si-s	sis
si	si-p	sip
bi	bi-t	bit
wi	wi-g	wig
fi	fi-n	fin

Oo

to	to-t	tot
mo	mo-p	mop
ro	ro-t	rot
ho	ho-t	hot
do	do-t	dot

Uu

pu	pu-p	pup
pu	pu-s	pus
su	su-n	sun
ru	ru-n	run
du	du-g	dug

THREE-LETTER WORD REVIEW

sun fun	sad lad	mad dad
wet net	red bed	big fig
mop top	nip zip	let bet
nun run	bit sit	hot rod
get jet	fat hat	pig dig
rug bug	bum hum	pup sup
tip top	lip sip	ham jam

Review these words once a day -- first read them, and then write them, until it is easy for you. Take your TIME, and DON'T WORRY about making a MISTAKE.

. . . Remember . . .

It's NOT whether you stumble or fall that matters . . .

. . . what MATTERS is that you GET UP

and K E E P O N G O I N G !!!

The TWO SHORTEST WORDS in the English language are "I" and "a." You simply name the letter -- and THAT is the WORD!

Let's try reading "I" and "a," together with a few of the three-letter words you are now able to read.

Read down each group:

I get.
I get wet.

I bet.
I bet Dad.

I sip.
I sip pop.

I had.
I had fun.

I dug.
I dug mud.

I hug.
I hug Mom.

I tug.
I tug a pup.

I pop.
I pop a bag.

I got.
I got a pen.

I fed.
I fed a pig.

I ran.
I ran a bit.

I sit.
I sit a lot.

Read across the page:

hug pup	I hug a pup.
wet pup	I hug a wet pup.
big pup	I hug a big, wet pup!
had pig	I had a pig.
fat pig	I had a fat pig.
big pig	I had a big, fat pig!
hit bug	I hit a bug.
red bug	I hit a red bug.
big bug	I hit a big, red bug!

To avoid that RUN DOWN feeling . . . CROSS STREETS CAREFULLY!

jog bit	I jog a bit.
hop lot	I hop a lot.
	I jog a bit and hop a lot!
mop bit	I mop a bit.
yak lot	I yak a lot.
	I mop a bit and yak a lot!
sip bit	I sip a bit.
sup lot	I sup a lot.
	I sip a bit and sup a lot!

"K-C-CK"

The "k" sound can be spelled THREE DIFFERENT WAYS!

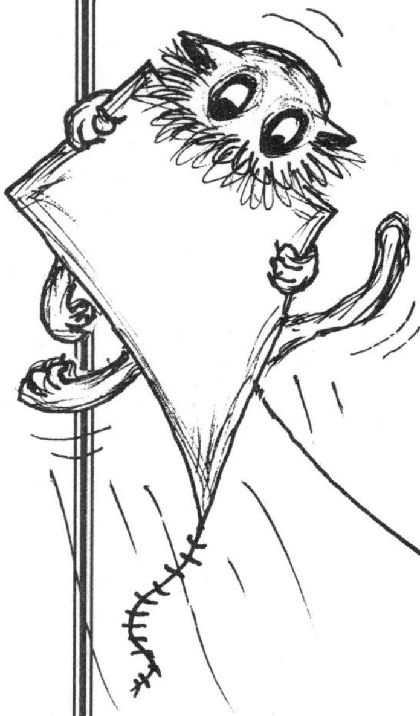

At the BEGINNING of a word it is spelled with a "k" if either "e" or "i" follow it, as in "KITE." Before ANY OTHER vowel it is spelled with a "c," as in "CAT."

Kk Cc

a	c-a	ca
e	k-e	ke
i	k-i	ki
o	c-o	co
u	c-u	cu

It's "k" and not "c"
with an "i" or an "e!"

cu co ki ke ca

ki ca cu co

Read down each set of words:

ca-t	cat	ke-g	keg
ca-n	can	Ke-n	Ken
ca-p	cap		
ca-d	cad	ki-d	kid
ca-b	cab	ki-ss	kiss
ca-m	cam	ki-t	kit
co-p	cop	cu-p	cup
co-t	cot	cu-t	cut
co-d	cod	cu-b	cub

Read across the page:

can	cat	cap	cab	Cass
keg	Ken	cad	cup	cop
kit	kiss	Kim	kid	kill
cod	cot	cop	cob	cog
cub	cud	cuss	cuff	cut

Ken cup kid Cass

cut can kiss cat

The "k" sound at the END of a word is usually spelled "ck." This is especially true when the word has only one syllable. Read across the page.

-ck

Many people find it helpful to hold a piece of paper underneath the line of words they are reading. Try it -- you may like it! Continue doing this throughout the book for as long as you need to, if it IS helpful.

so-ck	sock	sa-ck	sack
ti-ck	tick	to-ck	tock
du-ck	duck	su-ck	suck
bu-ck	buck	lu-ck	luck
Ri-ck	Rick	Di-ck	Dick
pi-ck	pick	Ni-ck	Nick
Ja-ck	Jack	pa-ck	pack
ra-ck	rack	ro-ck	rock

rack	Jack	back	sack	hack	lack
deck	beck	peck	neck	peck	deck
pick	sick	tick	Nick	Dick	lick
rock	sock	dock	hock	lock	jock
suck	tuck	luck	muck	duck	buck

pick Dick back pack

duck peck rock deck

"K-C-CK" REVIEW

luck buck	hot rock	Jack pack
Rick kick	Dick sick	tick tock
big lock	kiss Cass	hat rack
lick cup	lack sock	suck gum
duck peck	rock deck	tuck Nick

cat deck	I had a cat deck.
pick duck	I pick a wet duck.
lock cab	I lock a red cab.
pack sack	I pack a big sack.

Review these words once a day. Read as many as you can, and then write them.
Do this until you are able to read each word EASILY and SMOOTHLY, and spell them CORRECTLY.

Do something EACH DAY, even though you may NOT ALWAYS FEEL like it.

Remember . . . a DIAMOND is really NOTHING

but a PIECE OF COAL that MADE GOOD

U N D E R   P R E S S U R E !!!

INTRODUCTION TO ENDINGS (SHORT-VOWEL WORDS) DOUBLE-CONSONANT ENDINGS

NOW we are ready for FOUR-LETTER words!

1. Working from left to right, say the two-letter blend, then the three-letter blend, and finally the four-letter word. You should be able to say the three-letter blend SMOOTHLY, and THEN add the last letter. Read, and then write, as many words as you are able to each day. (If this is too hard to do just yet, continue reviewing the three-letter words until you are able to read the four-letter words a little more smoothly.)

2. LISTEN to these words, and then WRITE them. (More advanced students may be able to write the whole sentences from dictation as well.)

3. Try reading the little "stories" in the bottom window. They contain only words you can figure out from lessons learned so far, B U T -- reading sentences requires a HIGHER LEVEL of eye tracking ability which you MAY or MAY NOT be ready for. If these stories are too hard to read just yet, then only read the words to the left of each sentence, and try to follow along with your eyes as your teacher SLOWLY reads these sentences and underlines each word with her finger. Then she will read this sentence again, and STOP at one of the words you have just read, so that YOU can read it. You will need to pay close attention, in order to see WHERE she will stop, and WHICH WORD you will be reading!

There are FOUR WORDS in these stories where the "s" sounds like "z:" "is," "his," "as," and "has."
Let's PRACTICE these words FIRST, in short phrases.
Read down each group:

is	his	is
is mad	his bed	jet is
is mad as	his bed has	his jet is
as	has	as
as hot	pup has	bad as
as hot as	his pup has	as bad as

Ss

sa	sap	
se	set	
si	sip	
so	sob	
su	sum	
sa	san	sand
se	sen	send

Mm

ma	man	
me	met	
mi	mid	
mo	mop	
mu	mud	
mi	mis	mist
mi	mil	milk

Ll

la	lan	land
le	len	lend
li	lis	list
lo	lof	loft
lu	lum	lump
li	lim	limp

Ff

fa	fas	fast
fe	fen	fend
fi	fis	fist
fo	fon	fond
fu	fun	fund
fe	fel	felt

Ben felt	Ben felt sand.
his sand	His sand is hot.
runs fast	Ben runs fast on hot sand.

Bb

ba	ban	band
be	ben	bend
bi	bil	bilk
bo	bon	bond
bu	bus	bust
be	bes	best

Rr

ra	ram	ramp
re	res	rest
ri	rif	rift
ro	rom	romp
ru	rus	rust
ra	raf	raft

Dd

da	dam	damp
de	des	desk
di	dis	disk
du	dum	dump
de	den	dent
du	dus	dust

Hh

ha	han	hand
he	hel	held
hi	hin	hint
hu	hus	husk
hu	hun	hunt
hu	hul	hulk

Ben kept	Ben kept a pet pig.
held Gus	Ben held Gus, his pet pig.
romp hunt	Gus and Ben romp and hunt.

Gg

ga gas gasp
gu gul gulp
gu gus gust

Tt

ta tas task
te ten tent
tu tus tusk

Pp

pe pes pest
pu pum pump
pe pen pent

Kk

ki kil kilt
ke kep kept
ke kel kelp

Jj

ju jus just
ju jum jump
je jes jest

Ww

we wep wept
wi wim wimp
wi win wind

Not EVERYONE at this point will need to read the two-letter blends first -- but they are here for those who DO need the practice. If you STILL TEND to REVERSE letters or words, then it is BEST that you practice your "EYEROBICS " and read each blend FIRST.

jump land	Ben and Gus jump on land.
just tent	Gus is just as fat as a big tent.
jogs pants	Ben jogs and Gus pants.

-mp

da	dam	damp
bu	bum	bump
ro	rom	romp
wi	wim	wimp
ju	jum	jump

-nd

fe	fen	fend
sa	san	sand
re	ren	rend
la	lan	land
le	len	lend

-st

bu	bus	bust
be	bes	best
mi	mis	mist
la	las	last
ju	jus	just

-ft

le	lef	left
lo	lof	loft
li	lif	lift
tu	tuf	tuft
gi	gif	gift

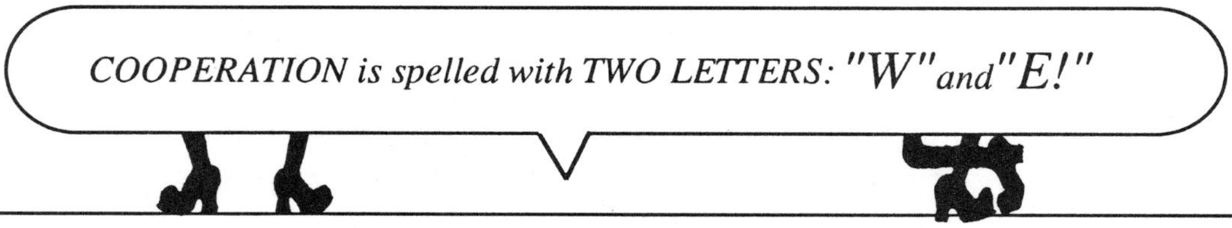
COOPERATION is spelled with TWO LETTERS: "W" and "E!"

Ben lifts	Ben lifts Gus on his lap.
just hulk	Gus is just a big, fat hulk!
mints milk	Ben fed Gus ham, jam, ants, figs, gum, mints, and milk.

-nt

de	den	dent
re	ren	rent
mi	min	mint
ra	ran	rant
le	len	lent

-lk

si	sil	silk
mi	mil	milk
hu	hul	hulk
bu	bul	bulk
bi	bil	bilk

-lt

fe	fel	felt
be	bel	belt
me	mel	melt
hi	hil	hilt

-ld

gi	gil	gild
we	wel	weld
he	hel	held

KEEP your TEMPER . . . nobody ELSE wants it!!!

jumps tub	Ben jumps in his hot tub.
went well	Gus went in his hot tub as well.
felt mad	Ben felt mad.
just jump	"Gus is just a pet pig. Pigs can not jump in hot tubs!"

-lf

el	elf
gul	gulf
sel	self

-lp

hel	help
gul	gulp
kel	kelp

There is NEVER a WRONG TIME to do the RIGHT THING!

-pt

kep	kept
rap	rapt
wep	wept
kep	kept

-sk

cas	cask
tas	task
bas	bask
tus	tusk

-sp

lis	lisp
gas	gasp
ras	rasp
wis	wisp

red bug	A big, red bug bit Gus.
tusks hump	It had big tusks and a hump.
wept help	Gus wept, "Help! Help!"
leg bump	His leg had a big, bad bump on it.
limp lump	Gus fell in a big, limp lump.
must rest	Gus must rest. His bump must mend.

Read across the page:

rom	romp	jum	jump	pan	pant
sen	send	mis	mist	hum	hump
min	mint	san	sand	ben	bend

Read down each pair of words:

damp	mint	silk	lift	sent
dump	hint	milk	sift	bent
rest	help	tend	wimp	lamp
rust	yelp	lend	limp	lump
rent	mend	must	land	raft
runt	bend	rust	sand	daft

held mints	Gus held ten big mints in his hand.
romps jumps	Gus romps and jumps on hot sand.
bends damp	Gus bends and gets a damp rock.
mints sand	His big mints fell on hot sand.
gulps mints	Gus gulps ten big sand mints!
felt sulks	Gus felt sick, and sulks a lot.

DOUBLE-CONSONANT ENDING REVIEW

went and bent	wimp is limp
camp is damp	yelp and help
duck has luck	kept and wept
hand has sand	milk and silk
rest and test	cask and mask
fist has list	hulk has bulk
lump on bump	tusk at dusk

sand and mist	lamp at dusk
jump on raft	big bent tusk
pant and rest	kept an elf
lift a duck	lend a hand
band is best	his mints melt
romp and jump	lump in milk
bend and sulk	hunt a hulk

Once a day, read and then write the words on this page. Do this until you are able to read and spell them EASILY.

You should be able to read these words WITHOUT having to sound out EVERY SINGLE LETTER FIRST. For example, if you find yourself reading "s-a-n-d" for "sand," cover up the last letter and read the three-letter blend first,"san-d," just as you did with the words on top of pages 46 amd 47. Continue reading words in this way until you are able to read them by blends and syllables automatically, if you DO need to break them up first. (Eventually you'll be able to just read them at a GLANCE without needing to break them up at ALL!)

It's IMPORTANT to continue using your BLENDING skills!!

"Y" ENDING

-y

Now we are ready for "y" endings.

Remember when we learned the five short-vowel sounds?
There is ANOTHER letter that is sometimes considered a vowel, too.

It is the letter "y."
When it is added to the END of a word, it has an "ee" sound.

When we add it to a word which has a DOUBLE CONSONANT ending, the spelling stays the SAME.

Sample: **mist** **mist-y** **misty**

H O W E V E R -- when it is added on to a word which has only ONE consonant on the end, we must add on ANOTHER consonant FIRST, in order to keep the SHORT-VOWEL SOUND.

Sample: **fun** **fun-n-y** **funny**

Read the words first, and then spell them from dictation.
Do this once a day.

Knowing rules such as this one will REALLY HELP your SPELLING.

There is NO SECRET OF SUCCESS except HARD WORK!

(There is only ONE PLACE that SUCCESS comes BEFORE WORK . . . . . . can you guess WHERE? Answer on next page . . .)

Here "y" is added to words with TWO-CONSONANT endings:

and	And-y	Andy
dust	dust-y	dusty
hand	hand-y	handy
rust	rust-y	rusty
sand	sand-y	sandy
milk	milk-y	milky
wind	wind-y	windy

dusty and rusty	jumpy and bumpy
handy and dandy	candy is sandy
silky and milky	lumpy and bumpy
Andy is sandy	Milly is silly
Kelly has jelly	dolly is jolly
hulky and bulky	pesty and testy

jumpy sick	Ben felt jumpy and sick.
pesty bug	Ben has a pesty bug.
bumpy bed	Ben rests on his bumpy bed.
Gus hid	Gus hid in Ben's bed.
lumpy bump	Gus is a fat, lumpy bump in Ben's bed!

 (Answer to page 49: In the dictionary!)

On this page, "y" is added to three-letter words with only ONE consonant at the end, and so we must DOUBLE this consonant to keep the short-vowel sound:

run	run-n-y	runny
pen	pen-n-y	penny
sun	sun-n-y	sunny
Dan	Dan-n-y	Danny
fun	fun-n-y	funny
Sam	Sam-m-y	Sammy
bun	bun-n-y	bunny

sunny and runny	Donny and Danny
nanny and Sammy	muddy and gummy
Jenny and Benny	funny and sunny
bunny is funny	Danny is sandy
Donny is muddy	Sammy is gummy

Some of these short phrases can actually be complete sentences. They are intended to be read as phrases, however, and therefore do not have any capital letters or periods.

Jenny fuzzy	Jenny has a fuzzy bunny.
bunny Sammy	Jenny's bunny is Sammy.
misty pond	Fuzzy Sammy fell in a misty pond.
funny muddy	Funny Sammy is muddy and wet!

"Y" ENDING REVIEW

Read across the page:

bitty	kitty	milky	silky
handy	candy	bulky	penny
funny	bunny	Henny	Penny
sandy	Andy	hilly	Billy
windy	misty	bumpy	lumpy
jazzy	Jenny	muddy	buddy

misty pond	I fell in a misty pond.
funny muddy	Gus is funny and muddy.
Jenny penny	Jenny has a rusty penny.
Andy kitty	Andy has a silly kitty.
dusty windy	It is dusty and windy.
lumpy rock	His bed is lumpy.

His bed is as lumpy as a rock.

Review as many words as you can once a day. Read them first, and then write them. Do this until you are able to read them S M O O T H L Y and write them C O R R E C T L Y.

KEEP ON GOING -- and never look BACK unless you want to GO that way!

TWIN-CONSONANT ENDINGS

Here's a NEAT TRICK to remember that will REALLY HELP your SPELLING! When a single vowel (usually one syllable) is followed by a final "l," "f," "s," or "z" we usually DOUBLE the letters in order to keep the SHORT VOWEL sound:

tell	fell	well	sell
will	hill	fill	dill
doll	loll	bell	dell

Biff	jiff	tiff	puff
buff	duff	huff	muff

bass	Cass	lass	mass
sass	Bess	mess	Tess
hiss	kiss	miss	fuss

jazz	buzz	fuzz	fizz

tell Bess	sell Puff	kiss Tess
bass mess	fell hill	sell jazz
Jess huff	fizz well	puff hill
fuzz mass	buff doll	lass tiff
miss Jeff	Cass will	sass Bess

Always THINK for YOURSELF . . .
. . . or SOMEONE ELSE will do it FOR you!!!

CONSONANT DIGRAPH ENDINGS

Now we are ready for something called CONSONANT DIGRAPHS.

So far, when we have had two consonants in a row, we have sounded out EACH ONE, as in "help." Both the "l" and the "p" get read.

Sometimes, two consonants next to each other make only ONE sound, that is DIFFERENT from either one:

Sample: "sh" (We say "shhhhh" when we want someone to be quiet.)

ru-sh rush ba-sh bash me-sh mesh

This kind of letter combination is known as a CONSONANT DIGRAPH. In this section, we shall practice reading these digraphs at the END of words. Every so often, just for fun, there is a "sneak preview" of what these digraphs sound like when put at the beginning of a word. More on beginnings later.

T E A C H I N G H I N T: When reading the words in these lessons, keep a list of the ones that are especially difficult. (There always are a few!) After you have read the whole group of words, go back to the difficult ones and read them again, carefully. Be sure to include them in your spelling as well -- writing them out will actually HELP make them EASIER to READ!

Some of you may not QUITE be ready to read the sentences in these lessons. Or perhaps you CAN read them, but it is VERY HARD. Unless you are able to read them FAIRLY EASILY, here is how to proceed:

1. *Read the two words to the left of the sentence. Have your teacher read the sentence to you while YOU move a finger SLOWLY across the sentence, underneath each word. FOLLOW her reading with your EYES, and when your teacher gets to each one of the two words you have just read, she will STOP and let YOU read each word to HER!*

2. *You and your teacher BOTH read the same sentence TOGETHER.*

3. *Now YOU read the sentence YOURSELF! (If you are ABLE to, that is. If not, only do steps one and two for awhile -- or even just step one.)*

Proceed in this manner for as many sentences in this book as you need to. At some point, sooner or later, you will be able to read them YOURSELF!

-sh

ba-sh	bash	ra-sh	rash
ma-sh	mash	sa-sh	sash
da-sh	dash	ga-sh	gash
ha-sh	hash	la-sh	lash
fi-sh	fish	di-sh	dish
wi-sh	wish	gu-sh	gush
hu-sh	hush	ru-sh	rush
ca-sh	cash	po-sh	posh

(sneak preview) sh-ip ship sh-op shop

dash cash	shop posh	rash gash
mash bash	fish dish	gush lush
lash sash	hush mush	wish fish
fish ship	posh shop	shop ship

FAILURE to PREPARE is PREPARING to FAIL!

dash cash	Let us dash and get cash.
shop ship	We can rush and shop on a ship!
wish fish	I wish I had a big dish of fish.

-th

pa-th	path	wi-th	with
ba-th	bath	ma-th	math
ha-th	hath	pi-th	pith
Se-th	Seth	Be-th	Beth

(sneak preview) th-in thin th-ump thump

path bath	Beth Seth
hath math	thin thump
thin path	Beth thump
with math	bath Beth

Beth math	Help Beth with math, Jenny.
Seth math	Seth can not get math.
Beth with	Beth runs with Jenny.
thin path	Beth runs with Jenny on a thin path.
thumps thin	Gus thumps a thin, red bug.

The SAME FENCE that shuts OTHERS OUT keeps YOU IN!!

"-SH, -TH" REVIEW

bash	bath	mash	math
rush	hush	dash	gash
wish	dish	path	bath
rash	hash	fish	Seth
hath	with	Beth	bath

fish mushy	His fish is mushy.
posh bath	Jan has a posh bath!
with math	Dad helps with math.
thin fish	Gus has a thin fish.
dash path	I dash up a path.
Beth wish	Beth has a wish.
rush path	Let us rush on a path.
mash fish	I mash his big fish.

Review these words until you are able to read them SMOOTHLY and spell them CORRECTLY.

Take all the time you need in order to do this easily.

And NEVER be afraid of making a MISTAKE!
After all, when you THINK about it, NOTHING would EVER be done at ALL if people waited until they could do it SO WELL that NO ONE could find FAULT!

-ch, -tch

This digraph is usually spelled "ch" if it FOLLOWS a CONSONANT:

pun-ch	punch	lun-ch	lunch
ran-ch	ranch	bun-ch	bunch
pin-ch	pinch	ben-ch	bench

EXCEPTIONS to this rule are: **rich** **such** **much**

When this digraph FOLLOWS a VOWEL, it is usually spelled "tch:"

pi-tch	pitch	fe-tch	fetch
ca-tch	catch	re-tch	retch
no-tch	notch	ma-tch	match
la-tch	latch	pa-tch	patch

Read across the page:

punch bunch	match patch	ranch lunch
catch latch	rich ranch	such lunch
much lunch	fetch bunch	bench notch
pinch match	catch match	punch bunch
retch lunch	patch bench	catch much

GOOD JUDGEMENT comes from GOOD EXPERIENCE . . .

. . . and GOOD EXPERIENCE comes from BAD JUDGEMENT!!!

"-CH, -TCH" REVIEW

Mitch pinch	Mitch can pinch and punch!
match catch	Can Ben match his fish catch?
fetch lunch	Mitch will fetch Jan's lunch.
hunch Dutch	He has a hunch Pat is Dutch.
pitch catch	Mom can pitch and catch well.
catch fetch	Catch his cat and fetch it lunch.
fetch punch	Fetch Gus lunch and punch.
match bench	A match fell on his bench.
catch ditch	His cats catch rats in a ditch.
munch lunch	Gus and Ben munch such a rich lunch!

There's a lot of
FREE CHEESE
in MOUSETRAPS,
but you'll NEVER find any
HAPPY MICE there . . .

GENERAL REVIEW

bash a bug	lunch at ranch
test is best	match his patch
Buddy is muddy	punch a bunch
pinch and itch	Henny Penny
latch a batch	gush and hush
fetch a match	such a lunch
Beth is thin	Pat is fat
Gus is fussy	catch big fish
dash with cash	rush and jog
jump and itch	bend a doll
pack a sack	yuck, bad luck
Jack on rack	cat has rat
Andy is funny	help and yelp

Review as many of these words as you can once a day. Practice READING them, and then WRITING them.

When you are able to read them SMOOTHLY and EASILY, and spell them CORRECTLY, you are ready to GO ON.

Take HOWEVER MUCH TIME you NEED . . .
. . . there is NO HURRY!
We are NOT RUNNING A RACE . . .
. . . we are L E A R N I N G H O W T O R E A D !!!

"NG" ENDINGS (ING, ANG, UNG, ONG)

-ing

s-ing	sing	r-ing	ring
p-ing	ping	w-ing	wing
k-ing	king	b-ing	bing
d-ing	ding	l-ing	ling

-ang

r-ang	rang	h-ang	hang
b-ang	bang	f-ang	fang
g-ang	gang	s-ang	sang

-ung

r-ung	rung	s-ung	sung
h-ung	hung	m-ung	mung

-ong

s-ong	song	d-ong	dong
l-ong	long	p-ong	pong
g-ong	gong	t-ong	tong

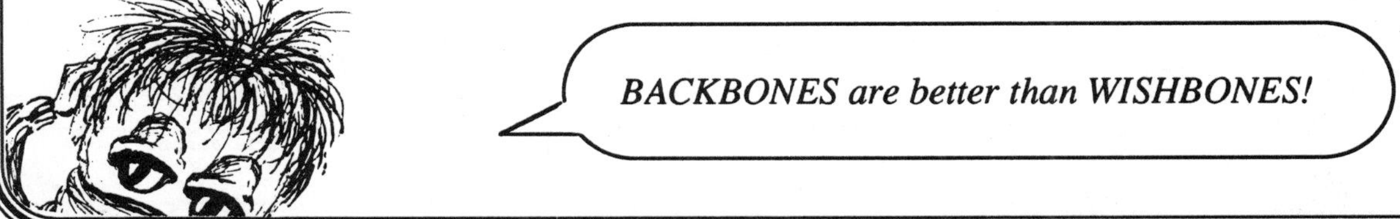
BACKBONES are better than WISHBONES!

"-ING, -ANG, -ONG, -UNG" REVIEW

Read across the page:

sing	sang	song	sung
ding	dang	dong	dung
king	kong	bing	bong
long	ring	fang	hung

sing song	ding dong	King Kong
gang sang	hung rung	long song
ping pong	king sung	wing fang

king sing	A king can sing.
King Kong	King Kong is big!
ping pong	Ping pong is fun.
rung hung	I hung on a rung.
Bing sing	Bing can sing well.
long tong	A fish tong is long.
sang rang	I rang and I sang.
gang fang	A bat gang had fangs.

LEARN from the OYSTER -- with a LITTLE GRIT he can produce a PEARL!!!

"-ING" AND REVIEW

fish-ing	fishing	help-ing	helping
wish-ing	wishing	dash-ing	dashing
bash-ing	bashing	limp-ing	limping
gasp-ing	gasping	jump-ing	jumping
bend-ing	bending	send-ing	sending
sing-ing	singing	mash-ing	mashing
rush-ing	rushing	gulp-ing	gulping

patching	matching	ringing	singing
packing	sacking	helping	yelping
sending	bending	itching	ditching
jumping	bumping	dashing	bashing

Andy rushing	Andy is rushing and dashing.
Ben helping	Ben is helping and packing.
Jan jumping	Jan is jumping and itching.
Pat singing	Pat is singing and fishing.
Gus gulping	Gus is gulping and munching a big, fat fish lunch!

The GREATEST MISTAKE you can MAKE in life is to be CONTINUALLY FEARING you will MAKE ONE!!!

"NK" ENDINGS (INK, ANK, UNK)

-ink

s-ink	sink	p-ink	pink
l-ink	link	k-ink	kink
r-ink	rink	w-ink	wink
f-ink	fink	l-ink	link

-ank

s-ank	sank	b-ank	bank
d-ank	dank	H-ank	Hank
r-ank	rank	t-ank	tank
y-ank	yank	s-ank	sank

-unk

s-unk	sunk	b-unk	bunk
d-unk	dunk	f-unk	funk
h-unk	hunk	j-unk	junk
p-unk	punk	h-unk	hunk

(sneak preview) ch-unk chunk

If OBSTACLES get in your way do as the WIND does -- WHISTLE and go AROUND them!

"-INK, -ANK, -UNK " REVIEW

Read across the page:

ink	sink	sinking	ink	link	linking
ank	bank	banking	ank	yank	yanking
unk	dunk	dunking	unk	bunk	bunking
ink	link	linking	ink	sink	sinking
ank	yank	yanking	ank	rank	ranking
unk	bunk	bunking	unk	junk	junking
ink	wink	winking	ink	kink	kinking

REVIEW -- reading and writing each of these words -- and then MOVE ON.

KEEP GOING! And remember . . .
ALL progress involves SOME risk . . .
. . . you CAN'T STEAL SECOND BASE
and keep your FOOT on FIRST!!!

Hank sinking	Hank is sinking fast!
pink bunk	His bunk is pink.
tank sunk	His tank sunk in a pond.
winking Hank	Jan is winking at Hank!
hunk sink	A hunk of ham is in his pink sink.

SIMPLE LONG-VOWEL SOUNDS

Up to this point, we have been building words using only short-vowel sounds.

NOW we are ready to learn some OTHER vowel sounds!

In this section, we shall learn the LONG sound of each vowel. In a way, these are EASIEST to learn, because the long sound of each vowel is simply its own name!

The diacritical mark for a long-vowel sound is a straight line over the top of the vowel, like this:

Āā Ēē Īī Ōō Ūū

The way we MOST OFTEN make a word with a long vowel sound in it is to add the letter "e" to the end of a three-letter word. The "e" we have added stays silent, but it CHANGES the short vowel sound in the word to a LONG vowel sound. It is often called the "MAGIC 'E'."

Here is how it works:

can can-e cane

We shall spend the next several pages reading words with long-vowel sounds, using the "magic 'e'."

As always, read the words first, then spell them from dictation. You probably KNOW to do this by now WITHOUT being reminded! Therefore, from now on we will not say it very often. Please remember to READ, and then WRITE the words in EACH SECTION for the *R E S T O F T H I S B O O K!*

Are there ever times when you feel AFRAID to TRY?
. . . You're NOT SURE you can DO it?

EVERYONE is. But it's ALL RIGHT to be afraid . . .
. . . It's only necessary that your COURAGE be just a L I T T L E B I T B I G G E R than YOUR FEAR!!!

Courage is RESISTANCE to fear and OVERCOMING it.
. . . It NEVER is LACK of fear.

Āā

Read down each set of words (can, cane, etc.). If it is too difficult at first to keep switching from short-vowel sounds to long-vowel sounds, then just read across each row first -- all the short-vowel words together, then the long-vowel words:

can	hat	cap	mad
cane	hate	cape	made
pan	fat	tap	gap
pane	fate	tape	gape
Sam	fad	bass	man
same	fade	base	mane
Dan	Jan	mad	ban
Dane	Jane	made	bane

Notice how the "ck" endings change to just "k" when "e" is added:

tack	Mack	back	lack
take	make	bake	lake
Jack	rack	sack	tack
Jake	rake	sake	take

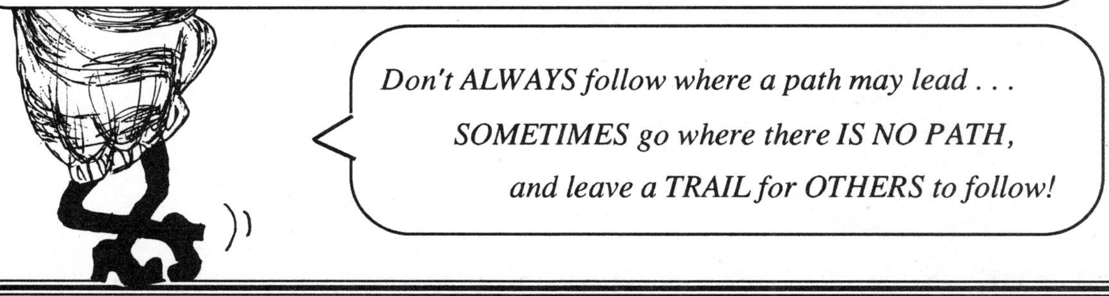

Don't ALWAYS follow where a path may lead . . .
SOMETIMES go where there IS NO PATH,
and leave a TRAIL for OTHERS to follow!

Read across the page:

bake cake	Jake rake	safe gate
late date	take game	hazy lake
made cape	rate Jane	mate wave
name tape	ate cake	fake pane

These words combine the long "a" sound with lessons previously learned:

cake sale	fish sale	duck sale
safe gate	ranch gate	cat gate
bake cake	rich cake	pink cake
bass lake	muddy lake	misty lake
pale Jake	catch Jake	pinch Jake

Jane bake	Jane and Jake bake a date cake.
ate hazy	Gus ate Jane's cake at a hazy lake.
Jake lake	Jake fell in a muddy, pale lake.
take fake	Take Ben's fake cat and name it.

I am only ONE . . . but I AM ONE!

I can't do EVERYTHING . . .

. . . but I CAN do SOMETHING!

ONE PERSON with COURAGE is a MAJORITY!!!

Īi

rip	hid	din	rid
ripe	hide	dine	ride
kit	pin	win	dim
kite	pine	wine	dime
bit	pill	fill	mill
bite	pile	file	mile
lick	pick	Dick	hick
like	pike	dike	hike

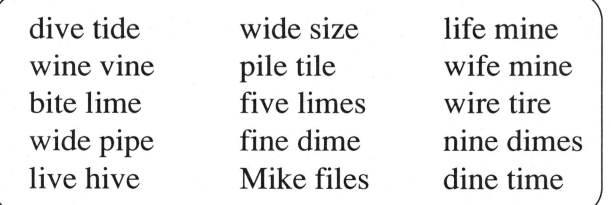

PEOPLE are like TEA BAGS . . .
They don't know their own STRENGTH
until they're in H O T W A T E R !!!

dive tide	wide size	life mine
wine vine	pile tile	wife mine
bite lime	five limes	wire tire
wide pipe	fine dime	nine dimes
live hive	Mike files	dine time

These words combine the long "i" sound with lessons previously learned. Read across the page:

bug bite	cat bite	duck bite
ride bike	take bike	with bike
dive tide	misty tide	pick tide
fine limes	bumpy limes	suck limes
mile hike	Jack hike	sang hike
live vine	yank vine	pinch vine
pile fish	pile sand	pile lunch
song time	dunking time	funny time
like Dick	like Hank	like jumping

time hike	It is time to hike five miles.
hide five	Hide his five dimes on his bike.
Mike ride	Mike will ride a wide tire.
fine wife	His fine wife is at his side.
likes bite	Gus likes to bite five limes.

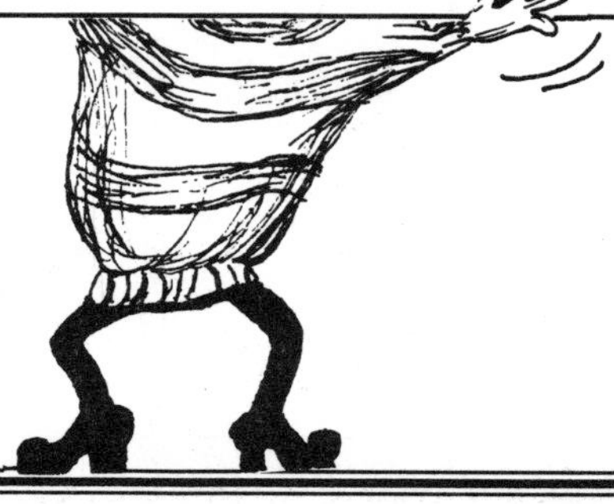
To treat your FACTS with IMAGINATION
is ONE thing . . .
But to IMAGINE your FACTS is another!!!

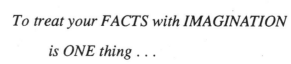

Ōō

hop	cop	mop	rob
hope	cope	mope	robe
tot	not	cod	rod
tote	note	code	rode
doll	lop	pock	jock
dole	lope	poke	joke

SPEAK WELL
of your enemies . . .
YOU MADE 'EM!!!

poke hole	lone sole	mole home
woke doze	hope joke	mope home
moles rove	note robe	woke home
pole dome	hole rope	rode home
tote bone	note vote	rove home
note joke	poke robe	lope home

Whenever you find yourself working TOO HARD over the SAME KIND of sound, go back and REVIEW that lesson. It is EXPECTED that this will happen from time to time. Some lessons need more reinforcement than others -- and EACH PERSON is DIFFERENT.

Reviewing what you have already learned is not only the BEST way to be sure you really know it well, but it is the ONLY way!

These words combine the long "o" sound with lessons previously learned. Read across the page:

big rope	patch rope	hang rope
neck bone	yank bone	such bone
pink robe	long robe	fetch robe
poke bug	poke Jack	poke Hank
rode fast	rode wave	rode raft
big joke	sick joke	nine jokes
pink home	like home	dashing home

mole pokes	A mole pokes holes in his home.
note robe	Note Jane's long, pink robe.
woke rode	Mike woke up and rode home.
tote bone	Tote a long bone on a bulky rope.
woke mopes	Gus woke and mopes in his robe.

There are TWO WAYS to say the long "u" sound, with a slightly DIFFERENT diacritical mark for each one:

Uu = yo͞o

cut	mutt	us	purr
cute	mute	use	pure

cute mule	use mule	cure mule
pure mute	cure cube	use cube

Uu = o͞o

tub	luck	duck	rub
tube	Luke	duke	Rube

rude June	rule Luke	tune lute
Luke duke	June rule	tube tune

ALWAYS think of how WELL you have done so far,
and that with EACH LESSON
you are a BETTER READER
than you WERE BEFORE!!!
. . . And PLEASE try to do SOMETHING

E V E R Y   S I N G L E   D A Y . . .

. . . The SMALLEST DEED is better than

the GRANDEST INTENTION!

These words contain BOTH long "u" sounds. When you SAY the word, you will SOON SEE WHICH sound FITS BEST!

cute June	pure tune	rude mule
use tube	mute rule	cure June
pure cube	cute duke	duke lute
use lute	June mute	rude duke
cure Luke	duke use	cute mule

He who KICKS CONTINUOUSLY SOON LOSES his BALANCE!!!

use June	Use June Lake -- it is pure.
tune cute	I tune a cute red van.
June tunes	June and Luke sing tunes.
duke rules	A rude duke rules back home.
use mules	We use mules to hike up bumpy hills.
Luke uses	Luke uses pure cubes in his cup.

GUESS WHAT? There are SEVERAL ways to spell the long "e" sound BESIDES just adding an "e" to the end of a short-vowel word. In this section we shall learn the "ee" and "ea" spellings of this sound as well.

("Ee" and "ea" are actually vowel digraphs -- two letters with one sound. We shall have more vowel digraphs later.)

Ee = ē

her	Ev	pet
here	Eve	Pete

ee = ē

(Read across the page:)

see	seek	seen	seed
fee	feet	fee	seem
wee	weep	weed	week
bee	meet	beef	beep
Dee	deed	deep	peep
heed	heel	peek	feed

SOMETHING TO THINK ABOUT: From now on, there will often be more than one way to spell a sound, with NO rules to go by at ALL! So you can see how it would be very difficult to learn how to spell these kinds of words while you are also learning how to read them!

In order to learn how to read as quickly as possible, it might be best to have each spelling group dictated separately, by "family," when you write these words, and then move on to the next lesson.

Later on, you can come back to these sections for more detailed spelling lessons. (It's also true that much spelling is simply "picked up" along the way, simply by reading books!)

ea = ē

sea	ea	tea
sea	eat	tea
seat	east	team
seam	each	teach

bea	lea	rea
beat	leaf	read
bead	lead	real
beak	leap	rear
beam	leak	reap
beach	leach	reach

There are THREE KINDS of PEOPLE in this world:
Those who MAKE things happen,
those who WATCH things happen,
and those who WONDER WHAT'S HAPPENING!

ear hear	heel feet	peep cheep
team teach	see bead	deep peal
seek peak	weak weed	gear here
near Dee	real peach	beast beak
reach peak	each bee	east beach

There are FIVE WORDS we must learn that have a long "e" sound that do not follow any special rules. They are:

me	be	he	we	she

feed me	eat weed	we see
be seen	be here	she eats
he reaches	we mean	near me
she leaps	teaching me	he seeks

These words combine the long "e" sound with lessons previously learned. Take time to review any rules that are especially difficult. Read across the page:

be here	be home	be lazy
feed me	feed Nick	feed fish
teaching me	teaching math	teaching Jack
lean beef	pure beef	rich beef
see me	wake me	ring me
kids leap	bunny leaps	Dee leaps
sink beach	fishing beach	misty beach
reach duck	reach latch	reach bunk
we treat	gulping treat	he treats

The WINNER says, "It may be DIFFICULT, but it's POSSIBLE!"

The LOSER says, "It may be POSSIBLE, but it's TOO DIFFICULT!"

feed neat	We feed each neat cat beef.
she eating	She is seen eating real meat.
reaches deep	He reaches in his deep seam.
each peals	Each bell peals near and clear.
leaps peak	He leaps on a peak near a beach.
weak peach	Feed me weak tea and a peach.
leaping each	See Pete leaping on each leaf.
Dee teaching	Dee is team teaching reading.
peeks beast	She peeks and sees the big beast.
leap each	See Gus leap and eat each bee!
weeds beef	Gus is eating weeds, bees, tea, beef, meat, and peaches.

JUST THINK of how FAR you have come!
. . . And always compare yourself
ONLY with the progress
YOU YOURSELF HAVE MADE . . .
NEVER compare yourself with OTHER PEOPLE.
. . . After all, if only the BEST BIRDS sang,
the WOODS would be SILENT!!!

LONG-VOWEL REVIEW (Read across)

cake sale	bake sale	bake cake	**a**
fake lake	name lake	hazy lake	
see beast	beach beast	see beach	**e**
Pete read	teach read	Pete teach	
wide dive	wife dive	wide wife	**i**
like Mike	bite Mike	like bite	
mope home	mole home	mole mope	**o**
tote note	code note	tote code	
cute June	rule June	cute rule	**u**
use tube	Luke tube	use Luke	

team teach	beast leaps	pure lake
cute deer	fake tune	make cube
take rope	neat joke	poke cake
hide me	we vote	five seeds
deep lake	rake weeds	ripe peach
we dive	he reads	she leaps
take bite	bake meat	cute Kate

LONG-VOWEL REVIEW

she read	She can read as well as Dee.
Luke takes	Luke takes a rake and weeds.
bikes home	She bikes home five miles.
each tiny	Each tiny mole is peeking.
hopes time	Gus hopes it is time to eat.
five bees	Five bees hide in a hive!
Pete pokes	Pete pokes a hole in a dike.
bite poke	He can bite, poke, and mope.
Eve dive	See Eve dive in a deep lake!
hikes miles	He hikes miles, and takes five cute mules.

FEAR less, HOPE more . . .
EAT less, CHEW more . . .
WHINE less, BREATHE more . . .
TALK less, SAY more . . .
HATE less, LOVE more . . .
AND ALL GOOD THINGS ARE YOURS!!!

There are a group of words that have a long vowel sound, even though they do not have an "e" at the end. Practice reading and spelling them.

old	sold	told	gold
bold	bolt	cold	mold
hold	fold	colt	jolt
post	host	most	so
roll	go	no	both

find	rind	kind	mind
tiny	hind	wild	mild

Ideas are FUNNY THINGS . . .
THEY don't work unless YOU DO!!!

mild post	old pony	cold jolt
kind colt	find gold	no colt
mind Mike	sold bike	hold cone
told joke	mile toll	ripe rind
fine mind	wild kite	most gold
so kind	go home	tiny colt
bone cold	Mike woke	old robe
lone colt	told Mike	so cold
no bite	old gold	kind Mike

These words combine long-vowel words without the "e" at the end with words from other lessons learned so far: Read across the page:

old pine	old fish	old duck
mild mint	mild Nick	mild lunch
so kind	so lucky	so much
pile gold	find gold	heap gold
wild colt	wild beast	wild deer
jolt home	jolt Beth	jolt Luke
cold colt	jumpy colt	running colt

go find	Go and find a big, shady old pine.
wild heaps	A wild man heaps piles of gold.
old cold	An old, old lake is cold and deep.
tiny mild	A tiny, mild colt folds its legs.
no both	No, both Ben and Andy can hold it.
find bold	We find Luke both kind and bold.

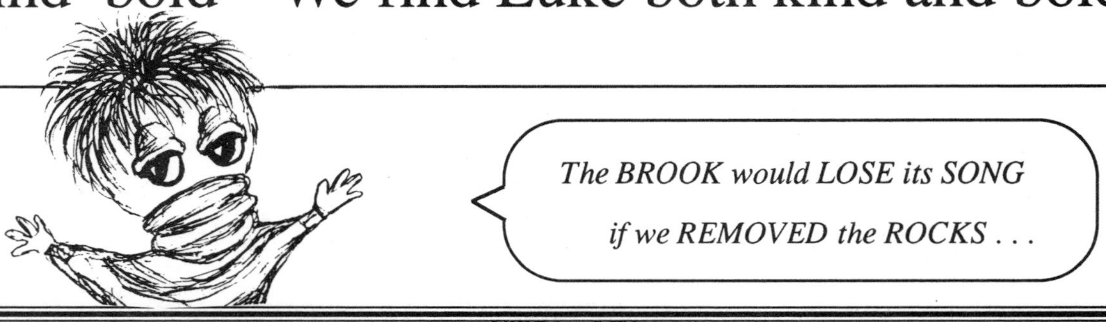
The BROOK would LOSE its SONG
if we REMOVED the ROCKS . . .

ADDING ENDINGS (SHORT AND LONG-VOWEL WORDS)
SHORT-VOWEL "ING"

On page 49 we learned that when you add a "y" to a word which has a short-vowel sound, you must add another consonant to the end in order to keep the short-vowel sound:

fun fun-n-y funny

We also learned you don't HAVE to add an extra letter if the word ends in TWO CONSONANTS:

mist mist-y misty

The IMPORTANT THING TO REMEMBER is that you almost ALWAYS have to have a double consonant following a short vowel when you put ANY kind of ending on the word. It doesn't matter WHAT ending it is! Let's try some"ing" endings:

hop	hop-p-ing	hopping
sit	sit-t-ing	sitting

Read across the page:

hop-ping	hopping	run-ning	running
kid-ding	kidding	rot-ting	rotting
set-ting	setting	bug-ging	bugging
hug-ging	hugging	sip-ping	sipping
sun-ning	sunning	tan-ning	tanning
hum-ming	humming	lag-ging	lagging
hit-ting	hitting	tap-ping	tapping

Of all the things you wear,
your EXPRESSION
is the most important!

SHORT AND LONG-VOWEL "-ING" AND "-Y"

What happens when we want to add an ending to a word, but we do NOT want the short-vowel sound? What if we WANT a long-vowel sound?

The long-vowel words usually end in silent "e." We simply STRIKE OUT the "e," and THEN add the ending.

Here are samples of "ing" endings added to long-vowel words:

ride rid-ing	bike bik-ing
cure cur-ing	take tak-ing
poke pok-ing	mope mop-ing
doze doz-ing	bite bit-ing
make mak-ing	hide hid-ing

Here are "ing" endings on both short AND long-vowel words: (Remember, short-vowel words must have a double-consonant before adding the ending!)

mopping	moping	hopping	hoping
ridding	riding	canning	caning
winning	wining	bidding	biding
tapping	taping	matting	mating
pinning	pining	ratting	rating
tacking	taking	backing	baking
racking	raking	licking	liking

Here are "y" endings on both short and long-vowel words:

ruddy	Rudy	furry	fury
holly	holy	catty	Katy

"ED" ENDINGS (SHORT AND LONG-VOWEL WORDS)

When we add "ed" to a word, it can be pronounced in three different ways:

-ed=ed

taste tasted	end ended	rent rented
fold folded	add added	land landed

-ed=d

name named	tame tamed	rave raved
save saved	wine wined	pile piled

-ed=t

bake baked	rope roped	kick kicked
kiss kissed	race raced	hope hoped

Of course, when we add "ed" to a SHORT-VOWEL WORD with only one consonant at the end, we must add ANOTHER one to KEEP the SHORT SOUND!

dim dimmed	cap capped	rap rapped
nag nagged	bag bagged	sip sipped
mop mopped	jam jammed	tug tugged
pin pinned	tap tapped	sob sobbed

Here are "ed" endings on both short AND long-vowel words:

pinned pined	licked like
tapped taped	hopped hoped
backed baked	mopped moped

"ED, ING, ER" ENDINGS

Long-vowel words:

taste	tasted	tasting	taster
waste	wasted	wasting	waster
poke	poked	poking	poker
save	saved	saving	saver

Short-vowel words with double-consonant endings:

kick	kicked	kicking	kicker
pack	packed	packing	packer
kiss	kissed	kissing	kisser

Short-vowel words with single-consonant endings:

mop	mopped	mopping	mopper
rob	robbed	robbing	robber
tug	tugged	tugging	tugger
yak	yakked	yakking	yakker

"-ED, -ER, -ING" REVIEW (SHORT AND LONG-VOWEL WORDS)

kicker	jammed	robber	yakked
nagger	baking	baker	kissed
yakker	tapped	tugger	taping
saver	dimmed	maker	kicked
taker	sipping	renter	dining

"ED, ER, ING" ENDINGS REVIEW (SHORT AND LONG-VOWEL WORDS)

hoping diver	We are hoping to see a diver.
jogging runner	A jogging runner kicked a can.
baker liked	His baker liked baking cakes.
saved piled	I saved lunch until it piled up.
racer sipping	See the racer sipping hot tea.
tasted bagged	Gus tasted as he bagged candy.
landed backed	A jet landed fast and backed up.
hissed robber	Kitty hissed and bit the robber!
wasted yakking	He wasted lots of time yakking.
licked munched	Gus licked, tasted, munched, gulped, and then felt sick.

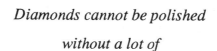

Diamonds cannot be polished
without a lot of
RUBBING and FRICTION. . .
and PEOPLE cannot be PERFECTED
without a lot of
TRIALS and CHALLENGES!

MULTI-SYLLABLE WORDS

SYLLABLES are the parts into which longer words can be divided. As a rule, each syllable contains a vowel and one or more consonants. When we divide long words into syllables, we HYPHENATE them -- that is, we divide them between each syllable with a dash. We ACCENT the syllable which gets the most emphasis by putting a slanted line over the top of it. The longest word in the world is easily read once it is broken up into syllables! Let's try just a few, so you can see how this works. First, say each three-letter blend below, one box at a time:

tic	tas	fan

Now let's read these syllables in a different order, and see what happens. Hint: the word is something that YOU are for having come SO FAR in this book!

fan	tas	tic

FANTASTIC!

lím-it limit
tíd-bit tidbit
táb-let tablet
in-ténd intend
in-súlt insult
tél-e-gram telegram
cáb-i-net cabinet

píg-pen pigpen
pár-ent parent
him-sélf himself
wít-ness witness
próf-it profit
ter-ríf-ic terrific
díf-fi-cult difficult

Just for fun, here's the LONGEST WORD IN THE DICTIONARY:

án-ti-dís-es-táb-lish-men-tár-i-an-íśm

Are there any special rules to use when we divide a word into syllables? Y E S! Short-vowel words are divided differently from long-vowel words. Let's take a closer look at HOW words are divided into syllables.

When dividing a SHORT-VOWEL word into syllables, the consonant usually FOLLOWS the vowel BEFORE it is hyphenated. It is a "CLOSED" division:

prof-it	cab-in	lim-it	par-ent
ex-it	rob-in	wag-on	prod-uct

When a short-vowel word has DOUBLE-CONSONANTS, we divide it BETWEEN these double consonants:

rud-dy	fuz-zy	mop-ping	hol-ly
pop-py	mud-dy	hop-ping	pen-ny

When we hyphenate LONG-VOWEL words, we divide them RIGHT AFTER the vowel. It is an "OPEN" division:

fu-ry	ru-by	Ka-ty	ho-ly
ra-ven	pro-gram	ha-zy	la-zy

EXCEPTION! Endings added to words are ALWAYS kept in their own little syllable. For example, we do not write "po-king" with an open division, even though it has a long-vowel sound. We keep the "ing" in a syllable by itself:

pok-ing	cur-ing	bik-ing	mop-ing
hop-ing	rid-ing	hid-ing	doz-ing
bik-er	rid-er	mak-er	bak-er

It's really nice to know this, because when you look up a new word in the dictionary, HOW it is DIVIDED will help you determine whether the syllable has a SHORT or a LONG SOUND!

When you spell these words from dictation, listen carefully to hear whether the vowel is SHORT or LONG -- then divide it CORRECTLY.

PLURAL, POSSESSIVE AND "X"

Plural means more than one. Most of the time we just add "s" to the word:

top	tops	duck	ducks
sing	sings	cat	cats
peg	pegs	hum	hums

With words ending in "sh, ch, tch, z," and "s" (also "x," which we shall learn on the next page) we must add "es" to the word. (This rule is easy to remember, because it SOUNDS different when you SAY it!)

batch	batch-es	gush	gush-es
fish	fish-es	fizz	fizz-es
inch	inch-es	kiss	kiss-es

Read across the page:

cans	dishes	pans	matches
jugs	wishes	mugs	batches
kicks	bashes	licks	catches
tops	rushes	mops	fizzes
pegs	fishes	kegs	quizzes
munches	bunches	punches	pinches
kisses	catches	matches	patches
racks	sacks	packs	backs
bells	balls	gushes	inches

You have TWO EARS and only ONE MOUTH . . . LISTEN twice as much as TALK!!!

When we add "s" to mean OWNERSHIP of something, we must first put an APOSTROPHE at the end of the word BEFORE adding the "s:"

Jan has a cat.	It is Jan's cat.
Ben has a fish.	It is Ben's fish.
Erin has lunch.	It is Erin's lunch.

When we wish to show ownership but the word already ENDS in "s," we only add an APOSTROPHE. We do NOT add another "s:"

Gus has candy.	It is Gus' candy.
Bess has a duck.	It is Bess' duck.
Les has a wig.	It is Les' wig.

The letter "x" sounds just like "cks." Read across the page:

tacks	tax	lacks	lax
Bix	box	lox	fox
Max	mix	fax	Rex
ex-it	exit	ex-ist	exist

NO PERSON is EVER BORN wise or learned!!!

Jan's box	Bess' wig	Bill's fox
Ben's pig	Erin's chick	Kate's home
Betsy's wish	ship's exit	Gus' lunch
Les' van	Mom's tax	Andy's bunny

GENERAL REVIEW

On the next page we start beginning blends. Before we do this, let's try a general review of what we have learned so far. If you find any endings here that you are a little UNSURE of, go back to that section and REVIEW them before going on.

First read the words, then spell them. Read across the page:

bath	bash	bask	back	batch
math	mash	mask	mack	match
with	wish	wisk	hack	hatch

suck	such	muck	much
Rick	rich	beck	bench
luck	lunch	buck	bunch
muck	munch	Puck	punch
sash	sack	rash	rack
bash	back	dish	Dick
handy	misty	beef	teach
king	fang	hung	song
mad	made	cut	cute

Gus' lunch	Erin munches	cute foxes
biking home	peaches hung	Les' duck
Pete punches	catching robber	Gus moped
colt biting	packing candy	runner puffed
yanking teeth	lacking film	penny sinking
humming tune	Sammy dozing	baking fish

CONSONANT DIGRAPH BEGINNINGS

Now we shall try putting some of the consonant digraphs we have learned at the BEGINNING of a word. The vowel sounds in these lessons will be both short AND long, so you MAY find yourself working a bit harder to read them! If you find you are working TOO hard over a sound (vowel OR ending) go back and review a few words on that page to refresh your memory.

Sh-, sh-

Read across the page:

sh-am	sham	sh-ame	shame
sh-ell	shell	Sh-elly	Shelly
sh-in	shin	sh-ine	shine
sh-ock	shock	sh-ock-ing	shocking
sh-un	shun	sh-un-ning	shunning

shall	shill	ship	shop
shin	shun	shot	shut
sheep	shape	shine	shone
shift	shifting	shack	shank
fish	shifty	mash	sham
posh	shop	shake	shock

shopped shaking mashed

Take your time! Do SOMETHING each day,
but DON'T be in a HURRY . . .
Sometimes the most BEAUTIFUL FLOWERS
in the garden are the ones that take
the LONGEST to GROW!!!

"SH-" REVIEW

hush ship	Hush, let us rush to his ship!
shot shin	Dan shot his shin bone.
such shock	It came as such a shock.
shall shank	Gus shall munch a sheep shank.
Shane shaky	Shane is in his shaky shed.
shift shine	Golden fish shift and shine.
shall shape	Shall we run and get in shape?
shift shake	Muddy land can shift and shake.
shiny shells	I shall get shiny shells to sell.
shine Shelly's	Sun will shine on Shelly's shack.

It's NOT where you STARTED in life that counts . . .

What MATTERS is WHERE YOU WIND UP!!!

Ch-, ch-

ch-ip	chip	ch-op	chop
ch-at	chat	ch-um	chum
ch-in	chin	ch-ug	chug
ch-ess	chess	ch-ill	chill
ch-eck	check	ch-uck	chuck
ch-ump	chump	ch-unk	chunk

Read down each group:

champ	chip	chat
chump	chipped	chatting
chug	check	chink
chugged	checking	chunk
cheat	chin	chum
cheating	inch	munch
cheer	chill	cheap
cheering	chilled	peach

No matter WHAT your lot in life may be . . . BUILD SOMETHING ON IT!!!

"CH-" REVIEW

Chuck chunk — Chuck chops a peach chunk.

chill chugs — Chad got a chill and chugs home.

chip chunk — This gold chip is a big chunk!

chomps chops — Gus chomps on chips and chops.

check cheery — Check the cheery, chiming bells.

chess cheap — Chuck's chess set is not cheap.

chubby chum — Gus is a chubby, cheery chum.

cheer chum — Cheer up a sad chum, and chat.

Chet chugs — Chet chugs and chases Gus.

chip-munk — A wee chipmunk chats and chats.

Kindness is the OIL
that takes the FRICTION
out of life.

Here's a NEW digraph blend! We haven't seen this before because it is only used at the BEGINNING of words:

Wh-, wh-

wh-en	when	wh-ip	whip
wh-eel	wheel	wh-ale	whale
wh-eat	wheat	wh-ich	which
wh-ile	while	wh-ite	white

which	when	wheel	while
wheat	whip	whale	white
whim	whine	whisk	whit

There are three words beginning with "wh" that we must learn by sight:

who   whose   what

A WINNER says, "LET'S FIND OUT!"

A LOSER says, "NOBODY KNOWS!"

Who is he?   Whose pup is that?

Who is he, and what is his name?

"WH-" REVIEW

whose white	Whose white wheel is that?
which whines	Which kid whines a lot?
what white	What is that white thing?
whose whip	Whose kid has a white whip?
which wheel	Which white wheel is rusty?
whine while	Ann and Dot whine while eating.
which whale	Which whale is big and white?
whose what	Whose cat is that, and what is its name?
wheat when	Gus eats wheat when he jogs.
while white	While we had a nap, Gus ate five white cakes.

A ship in a harbor is SAFE, but that's NOT what ships are BUILT FOR!

Th-, th-

The digraph "th" has two related sounds. The "softer" sound is like this:

th-in	th-ink	th-ank	th-ud
th-ump	th-atch	th-ick	th-ank

There is a SPECIAL diacritical mark for the "harder" sound of "th." (While it IS handy to know these marks, some students may wish to learn the rest of them them at a later time. They are not necessary to know right now in order to learn how to read, and can be learned later, if you like. But it IS NICE to KNOW them at SOME point!)

th = th

th-is	th-at	th-en	th-em
th-us	th-an	th-ose	th-ese

"TH-, TH-" REVIEW

this	thud	that	thin
than	think	then	thank
thus	thump	think	them
those	thing	these	thatch

There are two "th" words we use a lot, which must be learned by sight:

the they

The cats are lazy! They nap a lot.

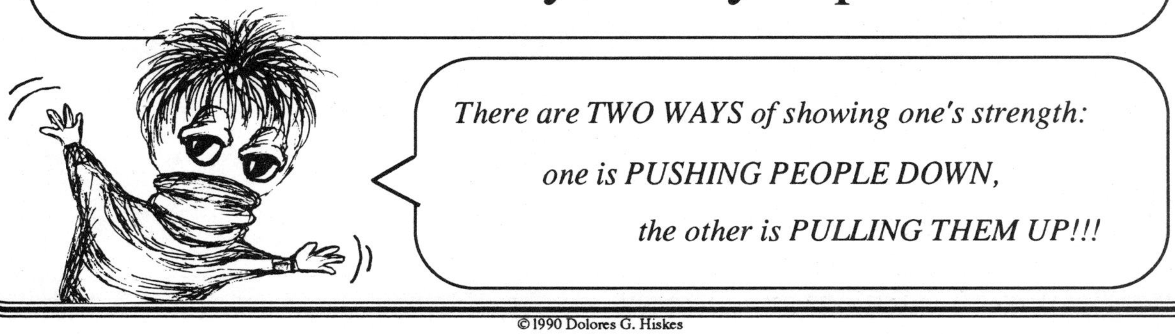

There are TWO WAYS of showing one's strength:
one is PUSHING PEOPLE DOWN,
the other is PULLING THEM UP!!!

"TH-" REVIEW

those thin	I think those thin cats need fish.
thing thumps	That thing thumps in the thatch.
thinks thick	Beth thinks this mud is thick.
Cathy the	Cathy takes the thick cake.
thuds thumps	Gus thuds and thumps when he jogs.
then thing	Then the thick thing went thud.
thinks thank	He thinks to thank them for the help with math.
thinks these	Gus thinks he can eat these big, thick, white cakes.
this they	This time they thank those thin kids.

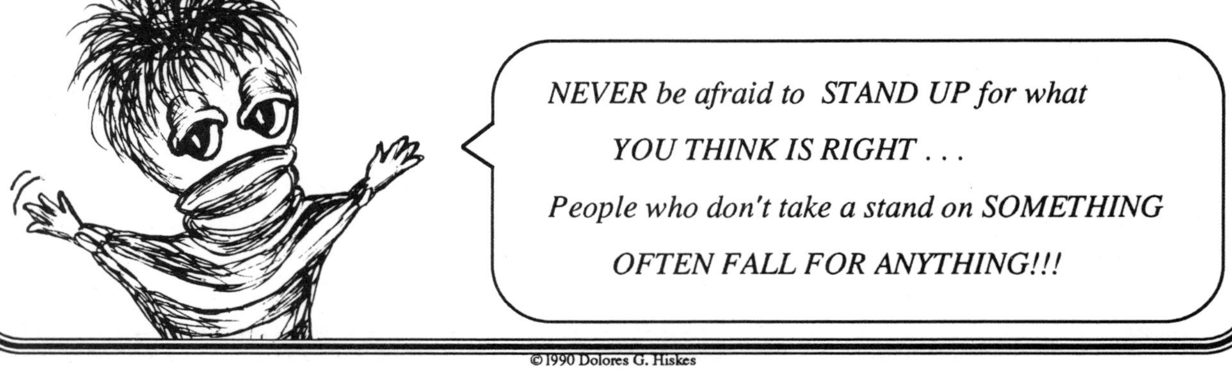
NEVER be afraid to STAND UP for what YOU THINK IS RIGHT . . .
People who don't take a stand on SOMETHING OFTEN FALL FOR ANYTHING!!!

Qu-, qu-

In the English Language, the letter "q" is always followed by a "u:"

qu-it	qu-ilt	qu-ick	qu-ack
qu-ill	qu-een	qu-eer	qu-est

quick quake	queen quacks	quit quest
quote quick	queer quilt	quick quack
quit quiz	quest quill	queen quit

quickly quake	Run quickly, it is quite a quake!
queen quacks	The queen duck quacks a lot.
quite quick	Dee makes quite a quick quilt.
quite queer	Gus thinks he feels quite queer.
quotes quite	He quotes quite a lot of things.
quit quiz	We shall quit this queer quiz.
quick queen	Quick, the queen feels quite ill!

As we grow OLDER, we are a LOT like PLANTS . . .
SOME of us go to SEED,
while OTHERS KEEP ON GROWING AND BLOOMING!!!!

CONSONANT DIGRAPH BEGINNINGS REVIEW

those white	Those white sheep can not cheep.
shaky shift	Shaky homes shift in a quake.
what quacks	What quacks in the thin shack?
quick shaky	Quick, get off this shaky wheel!
queer whale	That queer whale chased a ship!
shall quit	I think I shall quit this chess quiz.
that quilt	That white quilt is quite thick.
when queen	When shall the queen see them?
these chums	These chums chop thick shells.
who thank	Who shall we thank this time?
whose whine	Whose kids whine when shopping?
quit chubby	Gus quit chasing chubby sheep.

TWO PEOPLE looked at a rose bush:

one was ANGRY because the roses had THORNS,

the other was HAPPY because the thorns had ROSES!!!

DOUBLE-CONSONANT BEGINNINGS
"BL, FL, PL, CL, GL, SL"

Now we shall learn double-consonant BEGINNINGS. Read across each line. Not everyone may need to read all of the vowels and blends first, before reading the words. However, if reading is still hard for you, or if you still tend to reverse letters, then read ALL of the blends -- *DO YOUR "EYEROBICS!"*

bl-

a	la	bla	black
e	le	ble	bled
i	li	bli	blink
o	lo	blo	block
u	lu	blu	blush

black	bled	blink	block	blush
blend	bless	blip	blab	bluff

fl-

a	la	fla	flag
e	le	fle	fled
i	li	fli	flip
o	lo	flo	flop
u	lu	flu	flung

We
LOSE
GROUND
when
we
SLING
MUD!!

flag	fled	flip	flop	flung
flash	flesh	fling	flock	flunk
flap	fleck	flint	flog	flush

Practicing your "eyerobics" will make your eyes SO much stronger, and better able to move SMOOTHLY and EASILY across the page. Just as aerobics will make your BODY muscles a lot stronger, so that you can RUN faster!

pl-

a	la	pla	plan
e	le	ple	plenty
o	lo	plo	plot
i	li	pli	plink
u	lu	plu	plush

plan	plenty	plot	plink
plush	plum	plump	plant
plop	plus	plank	pluck

cl-

a	la	cla	clap
e	le	cle	clef
i	li	cli	cliff
o	lo	clo	clock
u	lu	clu	club

clod	class	clasp	clip	click
clinch	clench	cling	clang	clung
clump	clamp	clank	clack	cluck

gl-

a	la	gla	glad
e	le	gle	glen
i	li	gli	glint
o	lo	glo	glob
u	lu	glu	glum

glad	glen	glint	glob
glum	glass	gland	glib
glut	glop	glen	glad

sl-

a	la	sla	slam
e	le	sle	sled
i	li	sli	slid
o	lo	slo	slot
u	lu	slu	slug

We CAN'T turn BACK the clock . . .
. . . but we CAN
WIND IT UP AGAIN!

slam	sled	slid	slot
slug	slush	slap	slip
slum	slump	slash	slick

DOUBLE-CONSONANT BEGINNINGS REVIEW: "BL, FL, PL, CL, GL, SL"

flips flings	She flips and flings big blocks.
slid cliff	We slid on a big, black cliff.
please blot	Please blot that black ink fleck.
clench flash	Clench this flag, and see it flash.
flunk class	He shall not flunk this slick class.
fled flashy	He fled with the flashy clock.
clink clank	"Clink, clank, clunk," went his car.
Glen plops	Glen plops plums on his desk.
slip slide	I slip and I slide in the slick glen.
plenty plants	We see plenty of plants in class.
sleepy plops	Sleepy Gus slumps and plops into his plush, black bed.

If you are always giving others a PIECE OF YOUR MIND,
be CAREFUL that you DON'T PART with the LAST PIECE!

PALINDROMES

This page is just for FUN -- it's a PUZZLE! See if you can guess what a palindrome is. The answer is at the bottom of the page.

Clue: What do all of these words have in common?

pup	eve	dad
did	sees	noon
deed	peep	toot
lev-el	civ-ic	kay-ak
level	civic	kayak
ra-dar	re-fer	mad-am
radar	refer	madam
re-pa-per	re-vi-ver	red-der
repaper	reviver	redder

It takes 72 muscles to FROWN
and only 14 to SMILE . . .
And BESIDES . . .
SMILING adds to your "FACE" VALUE!

(A PALINDROME is a word that reads the same BACKWARD or FORWARD!)

DOUBLE-CONSONANT BEGINNINGS
"SM, SN, ST, SP, SC-SK"

The DARKEST HOUR is STILL only SIXTY MINUTES LONG!!!

sm-

a	ma	sma	smash
e	me	sme	smell
i	mi	smi	Smith
o	mo	smo	smock
u	mu	smu	smug

smash	smell	Smith	smock
smug	smoke	smile	smear

sn-

a	na	sna	snap
e	ne	sne	snell (not a real word!!)
i	ni	sni	snip
o	no	sno	snob
u	nu	snu	snuff

snap	snell	snip	snob
snuff	sneak	snatch	snake
snub	snag	snide	sneeze

SPECIAL NOTE to students still reversing letters, or finding it hard to read: Please begin EVERY LESSON from now on by going back to one of the pages in this section and reading across one group of words, from the short vowel to the whole word. It will be a GREAT "EYEROBIC" WARM-UP!

st-

a	ta	sta	stack
e	te	ste	stem
i	ti	sti	stick
o	to	sto	stop
u	tu	stu	stuck

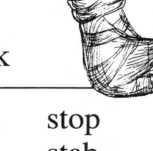

stack	stem	stick	stop
stuck	staff	step	stab
stiff	stuff	stock	stand

sp-

a	pa	spa	span
e	pe	spe	spell
i	pi	spi	spill
o	po	spo	spot
u	pu	spu	spun

span	spell	spill	spot
spun	spit	spunk	spank
spine	spend	sped	speed

sc-, sk-

Do you remember when we learned (on page 36) that the "k" sound is spelled with a "k" when it comes before "e" or "i," and with a "c" when it comes before an "a," "o" or "u"?

The same thing happens when you put an "s" before the "k":

a	ca	sca	scat
e	ke	ske	sketch
i	ki	ski	skip
o	co	sco	Scotch
u	cu	scu	scum

The most BEAUTIFUL TREES in the WORLD
FIRST began COVERED with DIRT,
but they ROSE ABOVE it.
GROW WHERE YOU ARE PLANTED!!!

scat	sketch	skip	Scotch
scan	scalp	skid	scum
scant	skill	skin	skim
scale	scope	skit	scuff

DOUBLE-CONSONANT BEGINNINGS REVIEW: "SM, SN, ST, SP, SC-SK"

sneeze smell	I sneeze when I smell smoke.
fleas sneak	Fleas sneak and stab Skip.
sneaky snakes	Sneaky snakes slip and slide.
stiff snobs	The stiff snobs sniff and snuff.
spilled stink	Spilled eggs stink and smell.
snoop skip	Dogs snoop, skip, and snuff.
snatch stack	Snatch the stack of stones.
spill spot	The spill left a black spot.
spin skip	We shall spin, skip, and skid!
stop smug	Stop that smug thief. Scat!
spunky skunk	The spunky skunk stands still.
spends snacks	Gus spends dimes on snacks.

In LIFE, as in RESTAURANTS, we must SOMETIMES swallow things we DON'T LIKE . . . JUST BECAUSE IT COMES ON THE PLATE!!!

DOUBLE-CONSONANT BEGINNINGS
"BR, CR, DR, FR, GR, PR, TR"

There are now many more words on each page than there were in the beginning of the book. You will probably find that reading only part of a page is enough for one lesson. IMPORTANT HINT -- put a sheet of paper underneath the line of print you are reading so that you won't be distracted by all the material. It helps! Read down each column:

br	**cr**	**dr**	**fr**	**gr**	**pr**	**tr**
ra	ra	ra	ra	ra	ra	ra
bra	cra	dra	fra	gra	pra	tra
brat	crab	drag	Fran	grass	pram	tram
re	re	re	re	re	re	re
bre	cre	dre	fre	gre	pre	tre
Brett	crest	dress	fresh	Greg	press	trek
ri	ri	ri	ri	ri	ri	ri
bri	cri	dri	fri	gri	pri	tri
brick	crib	drink	frisk	grip	print	trim
ro	ro	ro	ro	ro	ro	ro
bro	cro	dro	fro	gro	pro	tro
Bron	crop	drop	frock	groggy	prop	trot
ru	ru	ru	ru	ru	ru	ru
bru	cru	dru	fru	gru	pru	tru
brush	crush	drum	frump	grump	pru-	truck

DOUBLE-CONSONANT BEGINNINGS REVIEW: "BR, CR, DR, FR, GR, PR, TR"

Read down each group of words: ("Brat, drat; crab, grab;" etc.)

brat	crab	pram	drag
drat	grab	tram	brag
Brett	dress	Greg	bred
fret	press	dreg	Fred
brick	drink	grip	trim
trick	brink	trip	prim
crop	frock	groggy	prop
drop	crock	grassy	slop
brush	frump	drunk	crust
crush	grump	trunk	trust
crank	tracks	britches	crunch
prank	cracks	crutches	brunch

I hope you're remembering to review the words in each lesson until you are able to read and write them easily.

And please remember ONE THING . . .

NOBODY'S PERFECT!!!

(That's why PENCILS have ERASERS!)

DOUBLE-CONSONANT BEGINNINGS REVIEW:
"BR, CR, DR, FR, GR, PR, TR"

crabby Fred	Crabby Fred drags and frets.
Brent drinks	Brent drinks milk in the grass.
trucks crunch	Trucks drop and crunch bricks.
frock fresh	A fresh frock is a dream dress.
Frank grumpy	Frank is grumpy and groggy.
Greg crave	Fred and Greg crave brunch.
Fran crutches	Fran drops her broken crutches.
trip grab	I trip, and grab the brink of the grim cliff.
Trudy frisky	Trudy is frisky, and prances and trots.

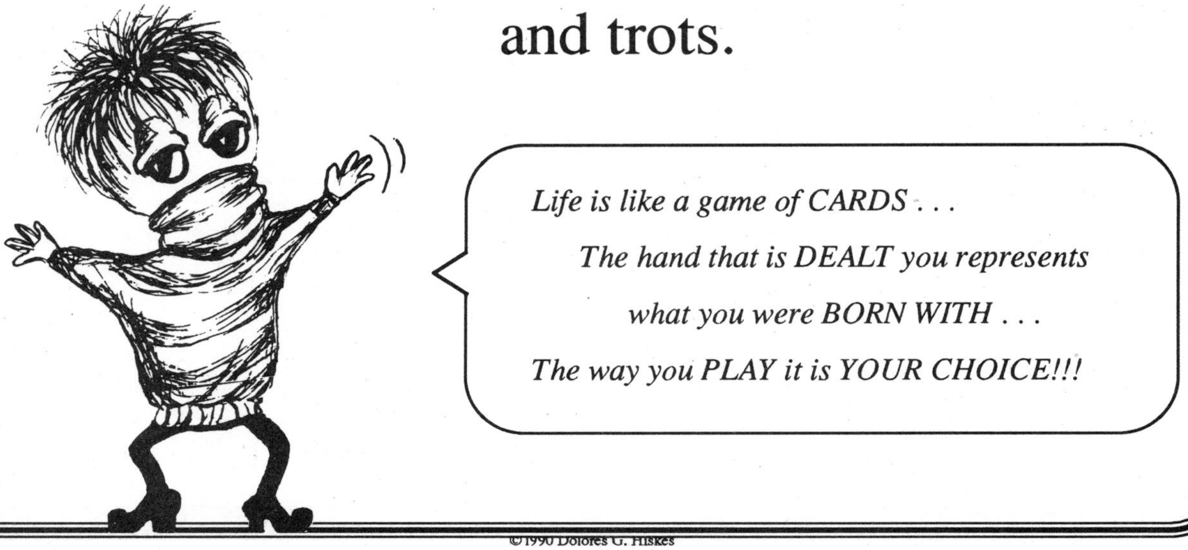
Life is like a game of CARDS . . .
The hand that is DEALT you represents
what you were BORN WITH . . .
The way you PLAY it is YOUR CHOICE!!!

GENERAL REVIEW -- DOUBLE-CONSONANT BEGINNINGS

Now we shall try longer sentences. Take it easy -- you don't have to read them quickly! These sentences are more complicated, so don't get discouraged if you slow down a bit when reading them. Everyone does. It is to be expected. HOWEVER -- if you are having TOO hard a time reading them, you may wish to go back to reading only PART of the sentence, as spelled out on page 54, or have your teacher read it first. The point is, you want to be C H A L L E N G E D -- but not F R U S T R A T E D!

snake glides	The sneaky snake slides and glides on the slick path.
sticky slinky	Smash this sticky, slinky, green slug. It clings to me!
grabs plenty	Fred grabs plenty of frisky, tricky, black ducks.
crabby groggy	Fran is crabby and groggy, and slumps into bed.
flung branch	Greg flung the branch in a clump of green grass.
glide swift	We glide, slip and slide with these swift skates.
sniffs brunch	Gus sniffs brunch, and drops his glass of fresh milk.

"R" MODIFIED VOWELS

So far we have learned about the two sounds vowels usually make -- the short sound, as in "rat," and the long sound, as in "rate."

When a vowel is followed by the letter "r" it makes ANOTHER sound, that is neither short nor long. This sound has been modified, or changed, by the "r." Practice reading, and then spelling, each word until you are able to do them easily. Read down each column:

ar = är (When you look up an "r-modified a" word in the dictionary it looks like this.)

ark	art	card	arm
bark	cart	hard	farm
dark	part	yard	harm
lark	mart	lard	charm
mark	dart	chard	yarn
park	tart	carp	barn
spark	start	harp	darn
shark	chart	tarp	parch
Clark	smart	sharp	farm-yard

yarn art	sharp yard	hard chard
charm Clark	dark park	farm barn
smart carp	start harp	chart park
lark dart	Mark bark	shark harm

FORGIVE and FORGET!!! SOUR GRAPES make BAD WINE.

"ÔR=OR, ORE, OUR, OAR"

or = ôr

(If you look up an "r-modified o" word in the dictionary it will look like this.)

Read down each column:

or	cord	sort	worn
for	cork	sport	torn
fork	corny	short	horn
pork	porch	snort	born
cork	torch	form	corn
stork	scorch	dorm	morn
story	north	storm	flor-ist
glory	forth	snor-kel	doc-tor

Take a lesson from the MOSQUITO . . .
It never sits around WAITING
for an opening . . .
IT MAKES ONE!!!

worn dorm	torch scorch	torn horn
stork snorkel	for florist	for doctor
sort corn	fork pork	born morn
short story	snort forth	corny glory
scorch corn	storm dorm	worn cork
north florist	doctor porch	snorkel story

There are THREE MORE spelling patterns for the modified "ôr" sound:

ore=ôr

core	tore	store	score
more	lore	shore	bore

our=ôr

four	pour	course	fourth

oar=ôr

oar	board	roar	soar

Here is a sentence using ALL FOUR spelling patterns for this sound:

Four storks soar on shore.

Copy this sentence over on paper, and circle each spelling pattern. Check to be sure you found them all. (It might also be fun to try writing another sentence, choosing your own words from each spelling pattern!)

pour more	court Dor	more corn
coarse pork	soar north	pour snort
four horns	worn board	short oar
for store	roar more	fourth dorm
soar shore	tore board	short course
four courses	wore more	four chores
more chores	four oars	fourth board

"ÄR" AND "OR, ORE, OUR, OAR=ÔR" REVIEW

four carp	Gus eats four carp, pork, corn, and a short shark for lunch.
chores before	Jan has more chores before she can dart and soar on a board.
horns yarn	The four horns are for Mark, and more yarn is for Clark.
doctor snores	The old doctor sits on his dark porch and snores and snores.
boards barn	The four boards in the dark barn are worn and torn.
course start	Of course she can take four more courses and start sports.
horse snorts	His big horse snorts, roars, and tore the cart in the yard.
smart sharks	Four smart sharks tore the oars on Clark's raft. Help!

To REALLY APPRECIATE the DIGNITY and BEAUTY of an OLD FACE, you have to READ BETWEEN THE LINES!!!

"ɄR=ER, IR, UR, OR, EAR"

There can be FIVE spelling patterns for the "er" sound! The diacritical mark for THIS sound is "ʉr." If you look up "her" in the dictionary, for example, it will show the pronunciation as "hʉr." (Read down each spelling pattern:)

er=ʉr	ir=ʉr	ur=ʉr
her	sir	urn
herd	stir	turn
pert	fir	burn
Bert	bird	hurt
jerk	birth	fur
term	mirth	cur
berth	girl	curl
Herb	dirt	curb
clerk	firm	purr
fern	first	lurk
perch	thirst-y	murk-y

her bird	firm dirt	pert girl
hurt cur	curl fern	Bert purr
first birth	turn berth	burn fir
fur herd	firm mirth	Herb clerk
jerk urn	curb dirt	firm turn
thirsty girl	murky fir	Bert lurk

It's what you LEARN after you KNOW IT ALL that COUNTS!!!

Here are two more spelling patterns for the "ur" sound:

or=ur

"Or" says "ur" whenever it has a "w" in front of it:

work	word	worm
worst	worth	wor-ship
world	worse	wors-en
worm-y	worth-y	wor-sted

ear=ur

earn	learn	yearn
heard	search	earth

Now here is a sentence using ALL FIVE "ur" spelling patterns:

Bert's earth-worms stir and turn.

Copy this sentence, and circle each of the five "ur" spelling patterns. Now try writing a different sentence, choosing your OWN words from as many of these groups as you can think of.

"ER, IR, UR, OR, EAR=UR" REVIEW

her work	Herb hurt	earn fur
girl turn	her word	Gert purr
early bird	dirty worm	first work
earth first	learn work	girl heard
worst burn	worthy urn	jerk perch
search world	thirsty fern	worm curl
worthy search	per-fect pearl	burn worsen

"ER, IR, UR, OR, EAR=UR" REVIEW

search stirs	We search for our pert kitty, Pearl. She stirs and purrs.
heard perfect	I heard Gert's work is perfect. She learns, and earns a lot.
yearns world	The girl yearns and searches for peace in her world.
earth-worms	Bert heard Herb will search early for his earthworms.
thirsty berth	Thirsty Herb curls and turns in his firm berth.
first learns	First, Gus learns to stir and turn his beef jerky. It burns!
Fern's dirty	We must first clean Fern's dirty but pert bird.

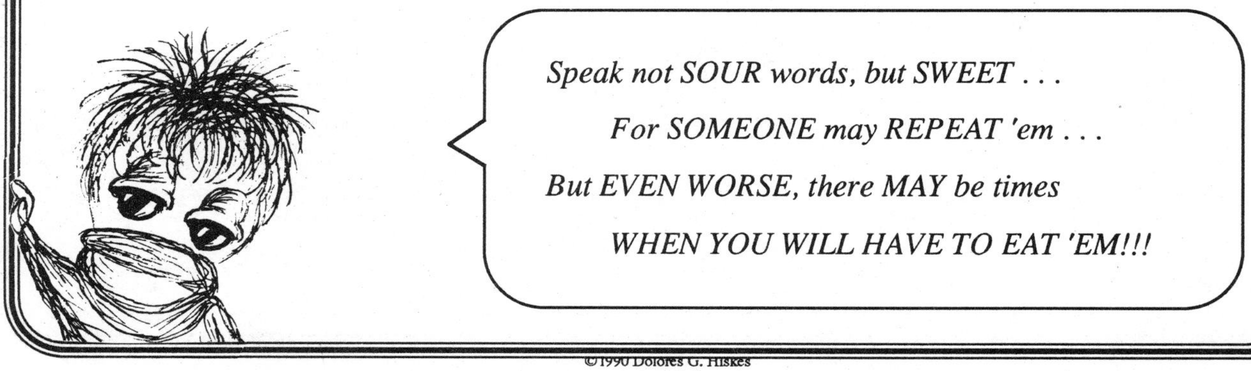
Speak not SOUR words, but SWEET . . .
For SOMEONE may REPEAT 'em . . .
But EVEN WORSE, there MAY be times
WHEN YOU WILL HAVE TO EAT 'EM!!!

Here is a review of all the "ur" spelling patterns -- they can be tricky to learn, and it's good to take time to know them. (Read down each spelling group:)

er	ir	ur	or	ear
her	sir	urn	work	earn
herd	stir	turn	worth	learn
pert	fir	burn	worm	earth
Bert	bird	hurt	world	heard
jerk	birth	fur	word	pearl
term	mirth	cur	worst	search
fern	girl	curl	worth	ear-ly
Herb	dirt	curb	wor-ry	search-ed
clerk	firm	purr	worth-y	learn-er
per-fect	first	lurk	work-er	search-er

her turn	firm dirt	pert girl
world search	earn pearl	Herb learn
hurt cur	perfect fern	Bert purr
first birth	early bird	worthy fir
worst herd	firm earth	Herb clerk
earthworm	girl worry	heard bird
jerk urn	curb dirt	worm curl
clerk learn	worker heard	searcher burn

SOMETIMES people are lonely because they build WALLS instead of BRIDGES.

Many longer, multi-syllable words contain these "r"-modified vowels, such as "ornament" and "performer." Let's try some!

hard	sharp	art
hard-en	sharp-en	ar-tist
hard-en-er	sharp-en-er	ar-tis-tic
car	form	su
car-pen	per-form	su-per
car-pen-ter	per-form-er	su-per-man
or	croc	al
or-na	croc-o	al-li
or-na-ment	croc-o-dile	al-li-ga-tor

If you find it difficult to read the longer words, try covering up most of the word first, and then SLOWLY move the paper over while you read each syllable. Some people find this helpful. What do YOU think? . . . . And, by the way,

DON'T just WAIT for your ship to come in . . . . . SWIM OUT to it!!!

hardener	sharpener	artistic
carpenter	performer	superman
ornament	crocodile	alligator

She is an artistic performer.
See you later, alligator . . .
After a while, crocodile!

LONG-VOWEL DIGRAPHS

The next section of this book will introduce some other ways to spell long-vowel sounds. We shall be learning the long-vowel digraphs.

A digraph, as you remember, is two letters that make one sound. We have had consonant digraphs so far, such as "sh" and "th," and we have also learned two long-vowel digraphs -- "ee" and "ea." Now we shall learn the rest of them.

It may take a while to learn how to read and spell these digraphs, so remember to take all the time you need with each one. As always, read and then spell from dictation all of the words listed.

As with the last section, the review sentences are longer and use more multi-syllable words. It is quite natural if you temporarily slow down a little bit when you read them. You are stretching and expanding your reading skills!

There is one thing you should watch for. If you find yourself really stumbling over the SAME KIND of sounds, then you need to go BACK TO THAT PAGE of the book and TAKE TIME OUT TO REVIEW it. It is common for this to happen, and is the true test of whether or not you know these rules well enough for them to be automatic when reading them. It does not matter if you are just slowed down -- speed comes with practice -- but you should not have to struggle with the individual words TOO much.

REMEMBER -- those whose eye tracking skills are still a little slow may prefer to continue reading these sentences the way it is suggested on page 54. And PLEASE remember to do your "eyerobic" warm-ups if it IS hard for you! (You didn't forget what they ARE, did you? Better check page 109.)

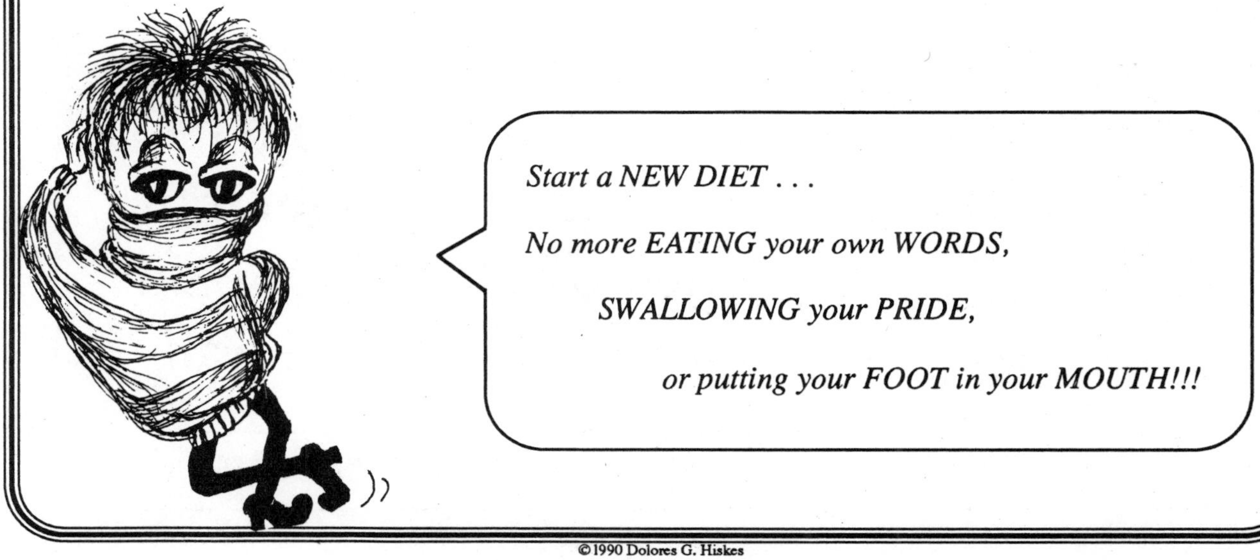
Start a NEW DIET . . .
No more EATING your own WORDS,
SWALLOWING your PRIDE,
or putting your FOOT in your MOUTH!!!

The "ai" and "ay" digraphs sound like long "a." Read down each column:

For many of these long-vowel digraphs,

there is an EASY WAY to remember how to read them:

"WHEN TWO VOWELS GO WALKING, THE FIRST DOES THE TALKING."

ai = ā

(This sound is spelled "ai" when it is in the MIDDLE of a word.)

aid	rain	ail	wait
maid	main	bail	bait
paid	gain	jail	trait
raid	vain	sail	faint
laid	pain	nail	saint
braid	Spain	pail	paint
aim	brain	Gail	taint
maim	drain	fail	stain
claim	train	frail	chain
plain	strain	trail	com-plaint

Gail braid	saint faint	paint train
paid maid	plain chain	maim nail
wait jail	stain rain	main trait
aim bait	brain drain	sail Spain
aid raid	laid pail	frail trail

Keep your FACE to the SUNSHINE, and you will NEVER SEE THE SHADOWS!

ay=ā

(It is spelled like this when it appears at the END of a word.)

Read down each column:

Jay	lay	way	ray
may	play	sway	pray
say	clay	a-way	gray
stay	slay	way-side	tray
tray	flay	mid-way	fray
stray	de-lay	day	bray
to-day	lay-er	day-time	hay
cray-fish	lay-away	holi-day	hay-stack

Those who bring sunshine into the lives of OTHERS cannot keep it from THEMSELVES!!!

gray day	Kay may	play clay
pay today	Ray betray	tray sway
spray hay	stray crayfish	May holiday

"AI, AY=Ā" REVIEW

gray rain	mail train	hay grain
clay trail	pay maid	frail Kay
slay tail	pail sway	say Spain
main trail	spray paint	gray day
aid crayfish	wait haystack	gray holiday

"AI, AY=Ā" REVIEW

Gail frail	Gail is frail, and must wait to play in the rainy bay.
mail train	The mail train is running late. Shall we wait at the gate?
tray crayfish	Gus laid his tray of gray crayfish on the main table today.
pay plain	Say, who can I pay for this plain gray cake tray?
Kay lays	Kay lays chains and nails in the pail on the clay trail.
paint gray	Please paint this ship plain gray. It will wait a day to sail.
Gail stay	Gail can stay late today. May we wait and play with clay?
trail freeway	Wait! I see the main trail faintly near the freeway.

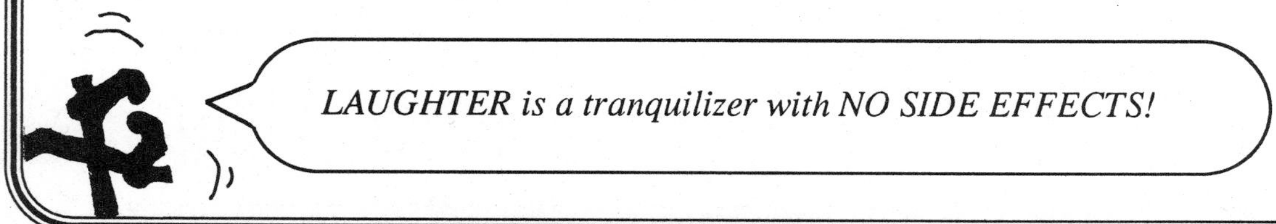
LAUGHTER is a tranquilizer with NO SIDE EFFECTS!

The "ie" digraph sounds like long "e." (We have already had "ee" and "ea" on pages 75 and 76.)

Read down each column: **ie=ē**

thief	pier	field
chief	tier	yield
grief	bier	shield
brief	grieve	wield
fierce	be-lieve	Deb-bie
pierce	re-lieve	Las-sie
priest	re-trieve	Ka-tie
fiend	a-chieve	Con-nie

A "y" ending is not a digraph, but is included here because it has a long "e" sound. (See page 49.) Also, when you make a word ending in "y" plural (more than one), you cross off the "y" and add "ies." Read across the page:

pan-sy	pan-sies	du-ty	du-ties
ru-by	ru-bies	pen-ny	pen-nies
ar-my	ar-mies	cook-y	cook-ies
par-ty	par-ties	ba-by	ba-bies
car-ry	car-ries	hur-ry	hur-ries
pup-py	pup-pies	kit-ty	kit-ties

slow-ly quick-ly wise-ly nice-ly shape-ly

"IE, Y=Ē" REVIEW

thief quickly	relieve Katie
carries cooky	shield puppy
Jackie achieves	Debbie slowly
chief armies	fiend hurries
party cookies	Lassie's babies
believe priest	carry pennies
Connie parties	achieve duty

Katie briefly — Katie and Debbie run briefly in the field of pansies.

hurry cookies — Hurry and carry ten cookies to baby Jackie.

believe priest — I believe the chief priest will be funny and brief.

carries tiers — Gus carries a party cake with cherries and ten tiers.

hand-ker-chief — Katie forgot her handkerchief. She quickly retrieves it.

The person who makes NO MISTAKES usually does not make ANYTHING!!!

Here "ie" has a long "i" sound. "Y" is not a digraph, but is included here because here it has the long "i" sound. Read across the page:

ie, y = ī

try	tries	dry	dries	fry	fries
fly	flies	cry	cries	sky	skies

lie	pie	tie	die
my	by	spy	spies
why	rye	eye	Clyde
type	typ-ist	style	styl-ish
ply	ply-wood	ty-coon	ty-rant
shy	dy-nam-ic	dy-na-mite	
hype	hy-per	hy-per-ac-tive	

To handle YOURSELf, use your HEAD . . .

to handle OTHERS, use your HEART!!!

spy tries	why lie	shy Clyde
dry tie	my eye	rye pies
try pie	why type	fly skies
by typist	my typing	spies crying
tyrant lies	shy Clyde	by plywood
dy-nam-ic style	sly tycoon	

"IE, Y=Ī" REVIEW

why Clyde	Why did Clyde cry? He tried to lie.
tried eyes	She tried flying the kite by my eyes.
tries fly	The fine jet tries to fly with style in the wild sky.
cried pies	Gus cried and cried while his fried rye pies dried.
dy-na-mite	Why did that spy try flying by Clyde's dynamite?
sly lie	The sly fox tried to lie by my vine.
shy typist	My shy typist has on a stylish tie.
die crying	Why did Clyde's fine, shy kitten die? He is crying.
tycoon lied	The sly tycoon lied, and tried to fly by my home.

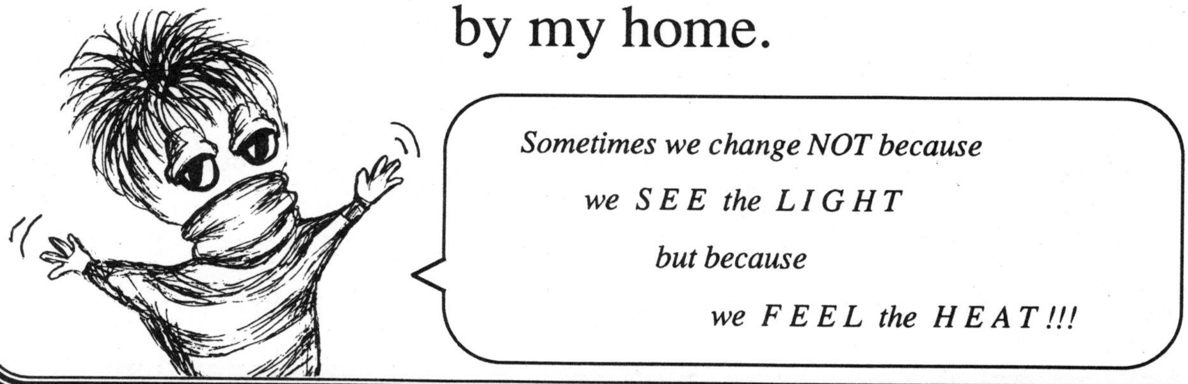
Sometimes we change NOT because
we SEE the LIGHT
but because
we FEEL the HEAT!!!

These sounds are all long "o." Read down each column:

oa=ō	**oe=ō**	**ow=ō**
oat	toe	tow
boat	hoe	bow
goat	foe	bowl
load	Joe	low
loaf	goes	slow
road	hoes	flow
roast	Joe's	grow

hol-low	yel-low	pil-low	win-dow
fol-low	fel-low	wil-low	sha-dow

toast loaf	coast road
soap floats	row boat
crow goes	roast oats
toad croaks	bowl slowly
hollow float	yellow hoe
low shadow	foam pillow
willow blows	show window
Joan follows	fellow goes
Joe's shadow	yellow bowl

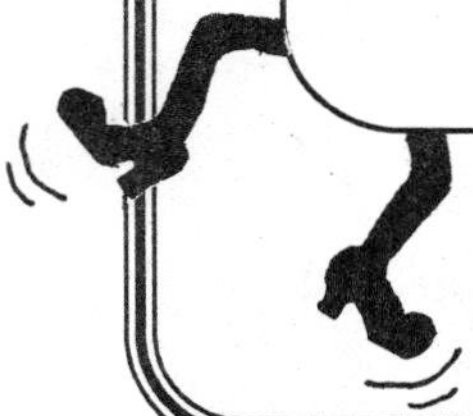
FAITH is what HELPS us LIVE BETWEEN the TRAPEZES!!!

"OA, OE, OW=Ō" REVIEW

boasts shows	Joan boasts, and shows her load of yellow bows.
loaf float	We like to loaf, float, and lie low in Joe's hollow boat.
flows slowly	This low river flows slowly until it goes by the coast road.
willow blow	These willow trees blow in the snow, and grow slowly.
follows grown	Joan follows Joe's grown goat. It goes most slowly.
show toad	Show Moe the old toad croak-ing on my yellow pillow!
roast loaf	Gus likes roast meat loaf, toast, and a bowl of oats for lunch.

Everybody has a FUTURE as well as a PAST. . .
Today REALLY IS
the FIRST DAY
of the REST OF YOUR LIFE!!!

These sounds are all long "u." Read down each column:

oo=$\overline{\text{oo}}$

moon
soon
spoon
tooth
goof
stoop
moose
zoom
fool
food
choose
drool
smooth

ew=$\overline{\text{oo}}$

new
stew
grew
drew
Lew
news
flew
mew
chew
dew
blew
brew

ue=$\overline{\text{oo}}$

true
glue
blue
flue
Sue
due

ui=$\overline{\text{oo}}$

A few words even have the long "u" sound spelled "ui!"

fruit	juice
bruise	cruise

ou=$\overline{\text{oo}}$

There are also a few words with the long "u" sound which are spelled "ou:"

you	youth	your	un-couth
soup	pouf	group	mousse

Here is a sentence using ALL FIVE spelling patterns for "$\overline{\text{oo}}$:"

New baby Sue drools fruit soup.

Copy this sentence and circle each one of these spelling patterns. Now write your own sentence, using as many "$\overline{\text{oo}}$" spelling patterns as you can think of.

"OO, EW, UE, UI, OU=O͞O" REVIEW

new moon	soon stew	chew food
goof proof	chew fruit	smooth cruise
moose drool	you choose	Lew drew
brew juice	Sue grew	fool tooth
fool snoops	moose soup	youth blew

goofy moose — The big, goofy moose grew blue under the new moon.

Sue drools — Baby Sue drools, and has a new pile of glue on her nose!

snoops blue — The moose stoops and snoops by the new blue pool.

smooth fruit — The smooth fruit juice is cool on Lew's loose tooth.

chooses cruise — Gus chooses a cruise with soup and food to chew, too.

Luke drew — Soon Luke drew a spoon with his new blue pencil.

Sometimes we HAVE to take a big step . . .
We CAN'T CROSS A CHASM in TWO SMALL JUMPS!

GENERAL REVIEW -- LONG-VOWEL DIGRAPHS

wait train	play train	wait play	
plain tray	clay tray	plain clay	a
frail trail	paint pail	maid paid	
Cain faint	plain rain	bait snail	
pennies field	shield field	shield pennies	
hurry kitties	kitty babies	hurry babies	e
grieve Lassie	thief yield	Connie carries	
puppies hurry	party cookies	believe Katie	
why pies	fry pies	try pies	
tried flying	tried drying	tried crying	i
tied spies	fried pies	dried pies	
trying fries	trying pie	flying sky	
coast boat	hold loaf	follow coast	
toad soak	willow grow	yellow pillow	o
Joe shadow	coast flow	load boat	
slow show	roast crow	fellow boast	
blue moon	choose fruit	smooth cruise	
fool Luke	moose soup	youth snoop	u
bruise Lew	goof proof	zoom soon	
choose news	grew tooth	fool drools	

"CE, CI, AND CY=S" (AND "EI" DIGRAPH)

On page 36 we learned that the "k" sound is spelled with a "c" when it is followed by "a," "o" or "u," and with a "k" when it is followed by "e" or "i."

What happens if we DO put "c" before "e" or "i?" It has an "s" sound!

ce

cent	cell	cel-e-brate
cer-ti-fy	cen-ter	cel-ery
cease	celebrate	ce-ment

When "ce" comes at the end of a word, the "e" is silent. Read down:

lace	race	rice
place	Grace	price
pace	trace	spice
space	brace	twice
prince	since	dance
prance	mince	dunce

The HARDER YOU WORK, the LUCKIER YOU GET!!!

space cent	prince prance	Grace celebrate
cease dance	trace cell	rice celery
center dance	dunce prance	cement place
dance twice	mince celery	race prince

ci, cy

civ-il cin-der cin-e-ma ci-der
cir-cus cir-cle cit-y cinema

"Cy" is usually pronounced with a long "i:"

cy-cle cy-clone cy-press

civil cinema cycle cinema cypress city
cyclone circle cinder cider circle circus

This brings us to our LAST LONG-VOWEL DIGRAPH. When the "ie" long "e" digraph has a "c" in front of it, the spelling usually CHANGES. It becomes "ei." Knowing this rule will REALLY HELP your spelling!

There is an EASY WAY to REMEMBER this:
"'I' BEFORE 'E' EXCEPT AFTER 'C'."

ei=ē

re-ceive re-ceiv-ing ceil-ing
con-ceive con-ceiv-ing con-ceit

receive ceiling conceive conceit

"CE, CI, CY=S" AND "EI=Ē" REVIEW

Grace receive	Grace will receive a price of ten cents for that lace.
horse prances	The black horse prances and dances in his center cell.
races receive	Gus races to receive his cider, celery and mince pie.
cycle cinema	Let us cycle to the cinema and see a circus film!
cyclone ceiling	The cyclone hit the ceiling and left a center space.
prince twice	The prince went to the dance twice to be with Grace.
cypress circle	Big old cypress trees circle that place in the city.
cel-e-brate fancy	Shall we celebrate and go to a fancy dance in the city?

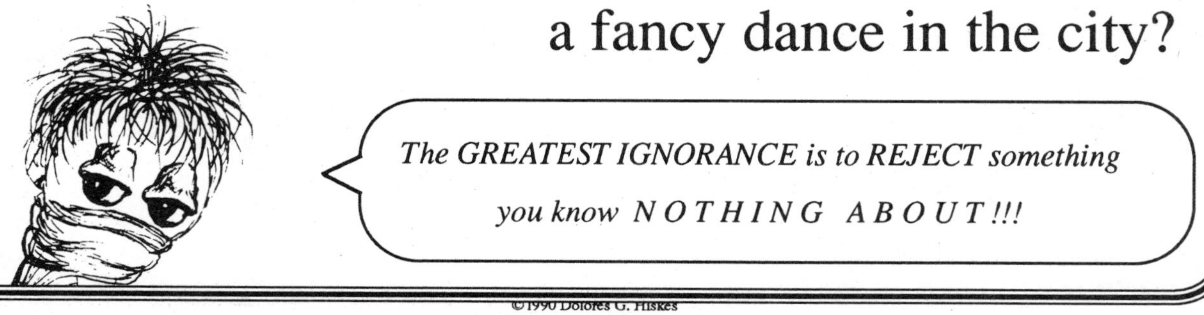
The GREATEST IGNORANCE is to REJECT something you know NOTHING ABOUT!!!

VOWEL DIPHTHONGS -- "OI, OY, OU, OW"

So far we have learned about DIGRAPHS -- two letters that make one sound. Now we shall learn about DIPHTHONGS. A diphthong is two vowels that make TWO sounds, but the sounds blend and slide together continuously to make a DIFFERENT sound. Let's try some!

There are TWO spelling patterns to the "oi" sound: "oi" and "oy."
The diacritical mark for the "oi, oy" sound is "oi." Read down each column:

oi=oi (This sound is usually spelled "oi" when it is in the middle of a word.)

oil	void	moist	coin
boil	avoid	hoist	loin
toil	noise	foist	join
foil	noisy	poise	joint
soil	broil	voice	point
coil	spoil	choice	oint-ment
poi-son	tin-foil	re-joice	ap-point-ment

Remember to read the longer words by syllables, covering up part of the word first if you need to *(see page 124).*
Or, simply put your finger under each syllable as you read it!

(Lessons are a little bit harder now, aren't they? Keep going . . . . . . ALL things are DIFFICULT before they are EASY!!!)

moist soil	boil oil	spoil choice
oil ointment	avoid poison	join tabloid
avoid noise	voice rejoice	point coin
appointment	broil tinfoil	noisy voice

oy=oi

(It is spelled like THIS when it comes at the END of a word.)

boy	soy	en-joy	Roy
Joyce	des-troy	con-voy	an-noy
toy	oys-ter	joy-ful	em-ploy

enjoy soy	annoy Joy	boy enjoys
toy oyster	joyful Roy	employ Joy
boys annoy	destroy convoy	enjoy oyster

"OI, OY=OI" REVIEW

boils soy	Gus boils eggs with soy oil.
Joyce coins	Joyce enjoys playing with Roy's toy coins.
noisy voice	Roy's noisy voice annoys Joyce, and spoils her nap.
spoiled oyster	This spoiled, green oyster is poison. Avoid it!
tinfoil enjoy	The boy broils his moist fish in tinfoil, and enjoys it.

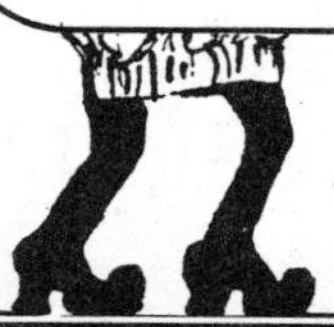

NEVER TROUBLE TROUBLE until TROUBLE TROUBLES YOU!

There are also two spelling patterns for the "ou" sound: "ou" and "ow."
The diacritical mark for the "ou, ow" sound is "ou." Read down each column.

ou=ou

(This sound is usually spelled "ou" at the beginning or in the middle of a word.)

out	ouch	bound	house
shout	couch	found	mouse
scout	crouch	pound	douse
trout	pouch	round	blouse
lout	slouch	sound	boun-ty
mouth	loud	hound	count
our	proud	wound	mount
sour	cloud	ground	fount
flour	foul	as-tound	a-round

NEVER be afraid of making a mistake, or failing.

FAILURE is NOT DEFEAT unless

you STOP TRYING.

ALWAYS REMEMBER . . .

Kites rise AGAINST the wind, not WITH it!

round ground	douse trout	loud sound
shout ouch	sour flour	found pouch
hound crouch	foul lout	cloud wound
proud mount	our hound	around couch
mouth sound	mouse house	astound scout

ow=ou

(Read down each column:)

This sound is always spelled "ow" when it occurs at the end of a word. It is also frequently found in the middle of words that have multi-syllables, or end in "l" or "n."

how	town	tow-er	owl
cow	gown	pow-er	fowl
now	down	cow-er	howl
vow	frown	flow-er	jowl
wow	crown	show-er	growl
pow	drown	glow-er	yowl
bow	brown	chow-der	scowl
vow-el	clown	pow-der	prowl
tow-el	crowd	browse	how-dy

Make YOUR life a LIGHT to OTHERS . . .
A candle loses NOTHING of its light
by lighting ANOTHER CANDLE.
Brighten the corner where YOU are!

howdy crowd	down town	flower power
owl frown	growl yowl	power vowel
how brown	fowl drown	crowd browse
brown gown	cower down	frown scowl
clown howl	crown power	shower towel

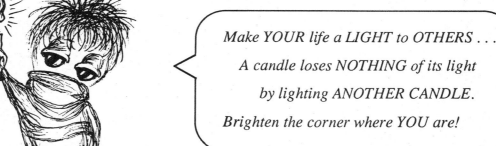

"OI, OY=OI" AND "OU, OW=OU" REVIEW

found tower	proud scout	town house
mouse growl	joyful choice	found towel
brown trout	moist oyster	round flower
avoid boy	noisy crowd	hound howl
frown ouch	shout howdy	annoy Joyce

boiled oysters — Gus found moist oysters and boiled them in soy oil.

ointment joint — Rub ointment on the sore joint and avoid a boil.

hound joyful — The hound makes a joyful howl in the toy house.

count brown — Did you count the brown, round trout in the lake?

proud scout — How joyful Roy is now at being a proud boy scout.

shouting frowning — Now stop the loud shouting, frowning, and growling!

LIFE is TOO SHORT to be SMALL!!!

"GE, GI, GY, DGE=J"

Whenever "g" is followed by "e, i, or y" it usually has a "j" sound. Read down:

ge, gi, gy=j

age	rage	cage	page
sage	wage	stage	huge
range	hinge	lunge	large
change	fringe	plunge	barge
gist	gym	gyp-sy	Marge

lunge cage	fringe stage	huge gym
Marge rage	hinge barge	large range
gypsy change	plunge stage	change page

change hinge — Please change the large, rusty hinge on that old range.

huge plunge — The huge cats plunge and lunge in the large cage.

Marge wage — Marge, please change my wage, and make it large!

lunge gypsy — They lunge at the huge gypsy on the stage in the barge.

It does NOT UNDO a mistake to ADMIT it, but it UNDOES US NOT to admit it!!

When "ge" comes at the end of a short-vowel word, if it only has ONE consonant before it we must add a "d" in order to keep the short sound. Read down each column:

-dge=j

edge	fudge	Madge	lodge
hedge	pud-y	badge	dodge
ledge	budge	badg-er	sludge
wedge	judge	ridge	trudge
pledge	nudge	ledg-er	smudge

edge ledge	Madge budge	judge lodge
pledge badge	smudge fudge	dodge ledge
hodge podge	pudgy Madge	hedge wedge

edge ledge — They trudge to the edge of the ledge on the ridge.

Madge dodges — Madge dodges the huge badger by the edge of the hedge.

pudgy fudge — Pudgy Gus gobbles huge wedges of fudge in the lodge.

hodge podge — His room is a hodge podge of sludge. He pledges to clean it.

A WINNER LISTENS . . . a LOSER just waits until it is HIS turn to TALK!!!

"GE, GY, GI, DGE=J" REVIEW

Madge charge	Madge and Sage charge up the edge of the ridge.
plunges large	Madge plunges off the large silver bridge near the lodge.
trudges lodge	Pudgy Gus trudges to the lodge for a huge plate of fudge.
badger wedges	The huge badger wedges himself under the stage in the lodge.
urge pledge	I urge you to pledge not to judge the change in Madge.
dodges gypsy	Sage dodges the gypsy and edges away from the large barge.
huge smudge	There is a huge smudge of fudge on the edge of that page.
plunge gym	The large badgers plunge in the hedge by the edge of the gym.

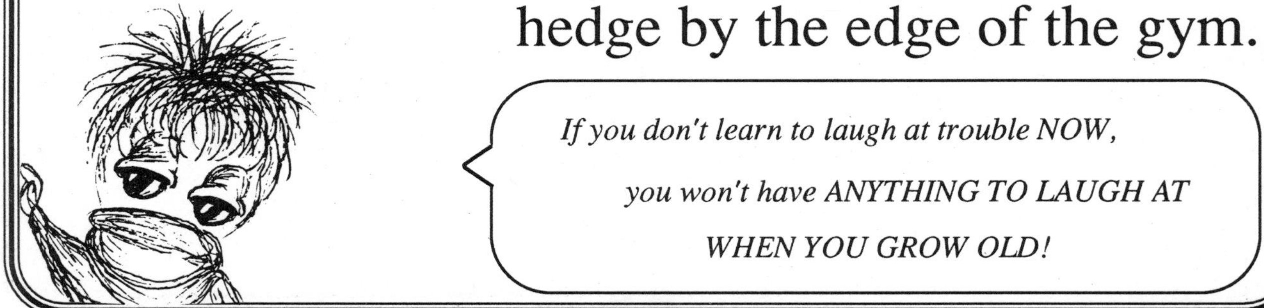
If you don't learn to laugh at trouble NOW,
you won't have ANYTHING TO LAUGH AT
WHEN YOU GROW OLD!

MORE ENDINGS: "Y=IES, IED, IER, IEST" AND "F=VES"

On pages 129 and 131 we learned how to make a word ending in "-y" plural -- by crossing off the "-y" and adding "-ies." For example, "cooky" becomes "cookies." The same thing is true for adding MOST endings to these words -- except for "-ing." Then it stays the SAME. Read across the page:

-y=-ies (etc.)

try	tries	tried	try-ing
dry	dries	dried	dry-ing
spy	spies	spied	spy-ing
cry	cries	cried	cry-ing
re-ply	re-plies	re-plied	re-ply-ing
de-ny	de-nies	de-nied	de-ny-ing
stud-y	stud-ies	stud-ied	stud-y-ing
car-ry	car-ries	car-ried	car-ry-ing

fun-ny	fun-nier	fun-niest
mist-y	mist-ier	mist-iest
bump-y	bump-ier	bump-iest
ear-ly	ear-lier	ear-liest

When a word ENDS with "-ie,"
we change "-ie" to "-y" before adding "-ing:"

lie	lies	lied	ly-ing
tie	ties	tied	ty-ing
die	dies	died	dy-ing

-f=-ves

When a word ends in "-f," to make it plural we usually change the "-f" to a "-v" before adding "-es." Read across the page:

loaf	loaves	wife	wives
leaf	leaves	elf	elves
life	lives	shelf	shelves
thief	thieves	wolf	wolves
be-lief	be-lieves	re-lief	re-lieves

"-Y=-IES, ETC." AND "-F=-VES" REVIEW

funny crying	funniest cry
reply believing	replying belief
earliest leaf	early leaves
wolf carries	wolves carry
loaf drying	loaves dried
thief lying	thieves lied
wife crying	wives cried
trying study	tried studying
wolf dying	wolves died
elf believes	elves believed
drying babies	dried baby
denied reply	denying replies

FEAR is the darkroom where NEGATIVES are developed . . .

"-Y=-IES, ETC." AND "-F=-VES" REVIEW

wolf carries	The huge wolf carries the five crying cubs down the hill.
wives believe	The wives believe the tiny babies are lying asleep.
replied loaves	He replied, "Gus tried eating ten loaves of pound cake."
leaves earliest	Leaves are earliest after rain, when sun tries to shine.
cried studying	They cried a lot, and then tried studying for the huge test.
believe funnier	I tried to believe that old joke gets funnier and funnier.
tried reply	He tried to reply that his shelves seemed the bumpiest.

It's not how HARD you FALL,
it's how HIGH you BOUNCE!!!

NEW VOWEL DIGRAPH SOUNDS
"OO=O͝O" (ALSO "OULD, U")

So far, we have only learned long-vowel digraphs. Sometimes a vowel digraph can make a COMPLETELY DIFFERENT sound! For example, "oo." We have had this digraph on page 135 as a long "u" sound, such as in "food." Now let's learn ANOTHER sound that it makes. Note the diacritical mark for THIS sound! Read across the page:

oo=o͝o

book	cook	cook-y	cook-ies
good	wood-en	hood	stood
book	brook	took	look
shook	soot	foot	foot-step
woof	roof	wool	hook

sooty cooky	good book	took hood
stood brook	wood foot	woof woof
wool hook	footstep	shook hoof
look book	stood foot	look cookies

look sooty	Look at that sooty wooden roof!
stood brook	We stood in the brook and shook.
good cookies	Look, Gus took ten good cookies!
cookbooks	Good cooks look at cookbooks.

An APOLOGY is a GOOD WAY to have the LAST WORD!!!

ould=o͝od

"Ould" is not really a digraph, but it has the same sound as the digraph we have just learned, "o͝o." There are only a few words with this combination, and this is a good time to learn them:

could would should

u=o͝o

There also are a small group of words in which "u" has this sound as well. When reading books later, if you are not sure what sound the "u" makes in a word try reading it with both the short "u" sound and the "o͝o" sound. You will soon see which fits! Read across the page:

pull	full	bull	bul-let
push	push-y	bush	bush-y
put	put-ting	pud-ding	pul-ling

"OO, OULD, U=O͝O" REVIEW

could put	should push	full bush
bushy hoof	would pull	put pudding
should push	bull could	bullet could
full bush	pushy bull	pulling bull
could push	should put	full pudding
would look	brook could	should cook
bullet shook	foot would	roof should

EXPERIENCE is not just what HAPPENS to you, it is what you DO with what happens to you!

"OO, OULD, U=ŎŎ" REVIEW

would cook	He would cook if he could just find a good cookbook.
stood putting	I stood and shook, putting one foot in the brook near the woods.
should look	I should look at that good book. Would you put it down?
took pudding	Gus took a good cookbook and cooked a pot full of pudding.
could push	We could put a hook on the hood, and push and pull it.
stood wooden	The good pup stood in the bushes on a wooden box. Woof!
pushed sooty	He pushed the sooty bull's hoof. It stood and looked mad.
look wool	Look, this wool is full of hooks!

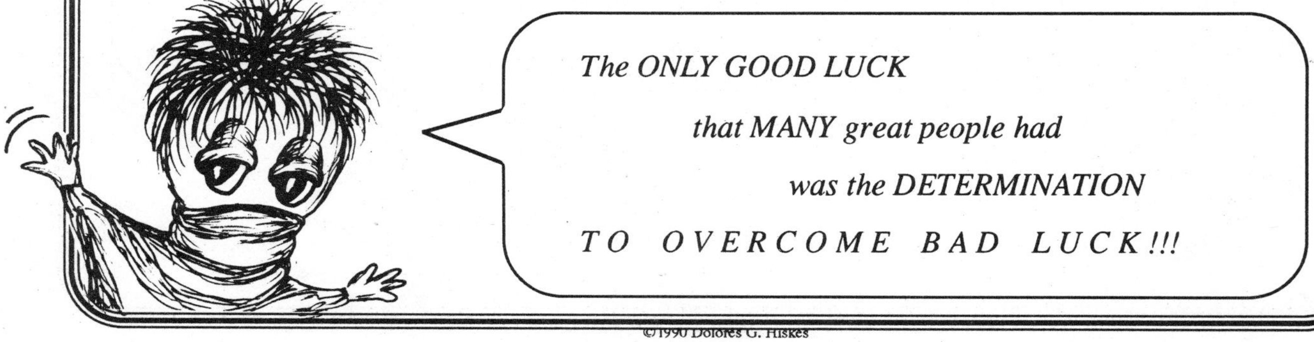
The ONLY GOOD LUCK
that MANY great people had
was the DETERMINATION
TO OVERCOME BAD LUCK!!!

"Ô=AU, AW" (ALSO "AL, ALL, O")

Note the diacritical mark for this sound. Try looking up one of these words in the dictionary -- "haul," for example, is shown as "hôl."

au=ô

Paul	pause	sauce	Maud
haul	cause	fault	clause

Paul pause	haul sauce	cause Maud
Maud fault	pause clause	Paul sauce

aw=ô

This sound is spelled "aw" when it comes at the END of a word. Read down each column:

saw	jaw	dawn	thaw
law	paw	yawn	crawl
hawk	draw	lawn	shawl

thaw dawn	crawl lawn	draw hawk
saw hawk	paw shawl	yawn crawl
dawn law	paw lawn	hawk crawl

Life must be UNDERSTOOD BACKWARDS . . .

but it must be LIVED FORWARDS.

Read across the page:

al=ôl

halt	halt-er	false	fal-ter
al-so	al-most	al-ways	salt
al-ter	al-ter-nate	bald	scald

also halt	almost halt	always halt
alter salt	almost bald	also scald
always falter	false halter	also alternate

all=ôl

all	wall	mall	fall
tall	stall	call	call-ing
hall	ball	small	small-er

all fall	small wall	stall ball
smaller ball	tall hall	wall hall
call mall	calling mall	small mall

It's NICE to KNOW that when you HELP someone UP A HILL you're a LITTLE NEARER THE TOP YOURSELF!

O=Ô

"O" is not a digraph, but in a number of words the "o" has the "ô" sound instead of "ŏ."

The sounds are very similar, but the name of something to eat will quickly show you the difference: "HOT DOG."

When reading books, if you are not sure which sound the word has try both -- one will fit. Read across the page:

dog	hog	fog	log
gone	smog	frog	lost
boss	cost	off	of-fer
soft	loft	floss	cross
moss	loss	toss	frost

"AU, AW, AL, ALL, O=Ô" REVIEW

small frog	dog paw	tall gong
false dawn	cross lawn	call dog
tall hawk	almost gone	call boss
salt hog	crawl fog	all sauce
frog yawn	always yawn	small fault
dog halter	lawn cost	lost shawl
Paul floss	Maude cross	crawl loft
soft dawn	hog sauce	moss lawn
also offer	frost thaw	saw smog

HARDENING of the H E A R T ages people MORE QUICKLY than HARDENING of the ARTERIES!!!

"AU, AW, AL, ALL, O=Ô" REVIEW

Please, PLEASE continue to TAKE YOUR TIME with each lesson. You are reading VERY WELL by now, but these lessons are more complicated, and take more time to read with ease. Remember this: professional football players or dancers are not good just because they already KNOW the game or the dance, they perform so well because they spend a LOT OF TIME practicing the things they ALREADY KNOW!

small yawns	His small pup yawns, and crawls on his paws to the ball.
hawk almost	We saw the small hawk almost fall on the frosty lawn.
lost hog	Gus almost felt lost when he saw all the roast hog for dinner.
all halted	They all halted and saw the soft pink dawn cross the sky.
frog draw	I saw a small frog I could almost draw, and also a dog.
always halts	Paul always halts and crawls on the tall, mossy log in the fog.
Maude offers	Maude offers almost all her cash for the small, soft dog.
Paul floss	Paul did not always floss, and he lost almost all his teeth.

THREE-LETTER CONSONANT BEGINNINGS

So far we have had double-consonant beginnings, as in :

cream	pray	trap

Now let's try adding ANOTHER consonant to the beginning of each word, and read some THREE-LETTER CONSONANT beginnings. Read down:

cream	pray	trap
scream	spray	strap
train	plat-ter	trip
strain	splat-ter	strip

thr-	**str-**	**scr-**	**spl-**
three	street	scream	splash
thrill	strip	scrap	split
throat	string	scrub	splint
thrash	strap	scrape	splin-ter
threw	straw	scratch	splat
thrush	stream	screen	splat-ter
throw	stroke	scram-ble	splen-did
thrown	strong	scruff	sprin-kle

We make a LIVING by what we GET . . .

but we make a LIFE by what we GIVE!!!

THREE-LETTER CONSONANT BEGINNINGS REVIEW

splash stream	spray street
sprinkle splatter	scratch scrape
strong splint	splendid scream
splatter stream	straw strap
threw screen	strain scramble
strain splint	strong splinter
scrub scrape	throw splat

splash splatter — The rain went splash and splatter on the screen.

scrape splendid — I will scrape and scrub this splendid cream on my plate.

scramble strain — See Gus scramble and strain up the hilly, scruffy street.

three thrash — Three flies thrash and strain in the strong bug strip.

splashed stream — I splashed in the stream with a string on a splinter.

splendid thrush — What a splendid thrill it is when the strong thrush sings!

Life is more FUN when you don't KEEP SCORE!!

SHORT-VOWEL SPELLING PATTERNS

ea=ĕ

On page 76 we learned how the digraph "ea" has the long "e" sound. Sometimes it can have a short "e" sound as well. Read across the page:

dead	read	bread
breath	deaf	head
heav-y	stead-y	read-y
weath-er	leath-er	feath-er
heav-en	leav-en	sweat-er
wealth	health	in-stead

ai=ĕ

In just a few words, "ai" can also have a short "e" sound:

a-gain	moun-tain
a-gainst	foun-tain

OPTIMISM is that CHEERFUL FRAME OF MIND

that enables a TEA KETTLE to SING

even though it's in HOT WATER up to its NOSE!!!

wealth again	feather head
heavy leather	health bread
ready breath	steady foun-tain
read again	heavy sweater
health in-stead	against moun-tain
leaven bread	leather again
heav-en-ly weather	mountain weather

y=ĭ

On page 83 we learned that "y" can have a short "i" sound when added to the end of a word. It can also have this sound WITHIN a word. Read across the page:

myth	myth-i-cal	crypt
lyr-ic	lyr-i-cal	cyn-ic
syr-up	typ-i-cal	sys-tem
Lynn	hymn ("n" is silent)	mys-ter-y
Flynn	Cyr-il	Syl-vi-a
cyst	hyp-no-sis	hyp-no-tist
lynch	gym	gym-nast
sym-bol	sym-pa-thy	syn-the-tic
crys-tal	cyl-in-der	hys-ter-ic

Lynn's syrup
Cyril's cyl-in-der
Sybil's myth
lyr-i-cal hymn
sym-bol-ic lyric
syn-the-tic syrup
sys-tem-a-tic gym
sym-pa-the-tic Lynn

typ-i-cal gymnast
mys-ter-y crypt
hyp-no-sis system
hys-ter-i-cal lynch
crystal cyl-in-der
cyn-i-cal Flynn
mys-ti-cal symbol
Sylvia's symp-tom

Even if you're on the RIGHT TRACK you'll get R U N OV E R if you just S I T there!!!

"EA, AI=Ĕ" AND "Y=Ĭ" REVIEW

health system	deaf cynic
Sylvia's feather	Flynn instead
heavy crys-tal	symbol wealth
steady foun-tain	typ-i-cal weather
read mys-ter-y	Cyril's sweater
against moun-tain	heav-en-ly hymn
mountain weather	syn-the-tic leather
sym-pa-thy again	hys-ter-i-cal Lynn

crystal foun-tain	The heavy, crystal fountain is ready again.
typical moun-tain	This steady rain is typical mountain weather.
Sylvia syn-the-tic	Sylvia already has a heavy, synthetic leather sweater.
typ-i-cal-ly syrup	Gus typically has a moun-tain of syrup on his bread.
heav-en-ly again	Miss Flynn sang the heavenly hymn again and again.

Did you know that more people R U S T O U T than W E A R O U T?

o=ŭ

At times "o" is pronounced with a short "u" sound. These words frequently have "m" or "n" next to them. Read across the page:

won	son	from	done
none	ton	mon-ey	hon-ey
oth-er	moth-er	broth-er	a-noth-er
lov-er	cov-er	a-bove	a-mong
mon-key	don-key	com-fort	Mon-day
shove	glove	noth-ing	some

one (wŭn) once (wŭns) of (ŭv)

ou=ŭ

In a few words, "ou" sounds like "ŭ:"

touch	young	cous-in
couple	double	coun-try

Sometimes even "oo" and "a" have a short "u" sound!

oo=ŭ

flood blood

a=ŭ

was (wŭz)

was from	once flood	above cover
love honey	one glove	another one
from cousin	was among	once mother
comfort son	nothing done	donkey was
double money	touch monkey	young blood
country cousin	young couple	brother shove

ə=ŭ

In multi-syllable words, the UNACCENTED vowel sound (including vowel digraphs) often resembles a short "u" in sound. The diacritical mark for this sound is "ə." It is called a "schwa," a German word which means silence instead of a vowel sound. It isn't REALLY silent, but is indefinite and neutral in sound. It certainly makes spelling a lot more complicated, since the "schwa" sound can represent ANY of the vowels! In the words listed below, the unaccented "schwa"-sounding vowels are underlined. (You may wish to just read these words for now, and learn to spell them later, after you finish reading this book.)

sofa	so-fə	(a=ə)
spoken	spo-kən	(e=ə)
sanity	san-ə-ty	(i=ə)
gallop	gal-ləp	(o=ə)
focus	fo-cəs	(u=ə)

Many words beginning or ending with an unaccented "a" have the schwa sound:

a-rise	a-woke	a-lone	a-way
a-while	a-void	a-round	a-cross
at-tack	at-tain	at-tend	at-tach
tu-ba	dra-ma	ex-tra	so-fa
so-da	chi-na	ze-bra	del-ta
for-mu-la	ba-nan-a	um-brel-la	va-nil-la

We also see it frequently with ending syllables, but the schwa can occur *anywhere!*

se-cond	for-ward	man-age	lem-on
sec-tion	teach-er	clev-er	fa-mous
pa-pa-ya	lot-ter-y	ve-loc-i-ty	dir-ect

You may find the WORST ENEMY or BEST FRIEND WITHIN YOURSELF!!!

"O, OU, OO, A=Ŭ" AND "ə=Ŭ" REVIEW

glove another	Bud lost his glove, but he got another one from Mom.
double banana	Gus just loves to munch a double banana nut soda.
nothing done	Nothing was done to stop the flood from coming.
monkey shoved	One month a young monkey shoved my brother.
once blood	Once some blood was taken from my other son.
loved touch	Mother loved to touch the fat, young, fluffy puppy.

A problem can be an O B S T A C L E or a S T E P P I N G S T O N E,

depending upon H O W W E S E E I T.

(Obstacles are those things we see whenever we stop looking at our goals!)

This sentence uses all short "u" spelling patterns. Copy it over and circle these sounds. Then write your own sentence, using as many of these spelling patterns as you can think of:

Once his young pup was running from a flood.

CONTRACTIONS

Here is an introduction to contractions. A contraction is what happens when TWO words are run together to make ONE word, and ONE OR MORE LETTERS are REMOVED from the second word. An APOSTROPHE is substituted for the missing letter(s). We use contractions as SHORT-CUTS when reading or speaking. Here is an example:

I am = Iam = I~~a~~m = I'm

~~i~~s = 's

she is = she's
he is = he's
it is = it's

~~a~~re = 're

we are = we're
they are = they're
you are = you're

~~wi~~ll = 'll

I will = I'll
he will = he'll
she will = she'll
we will = we'll
it will = it'll
you will = you'll
they will = they'll

n~~o~~t = n't

is not = isn't
are not = aren't
do not = don't
does not = doesn't
did not = didn't
can not = can't
could not = couldn't
was not = wasn't
were not = weren't
have not = haven't
has not = hasn't
had not = hadn't
should not = shouldn't
would not = wouldn't

CONTRACTION REVIEW

Read each sentence. Then name the ORIGINAL WORDS in each contraction:

She's sick.	We're going.
It's raining.	They're running.
You're limping.	It'll be fine.
He'll eat later.	We aren't afraid.
I wasn't kidding.	They weren't asleep.
Isn't Gus funny?	She doesn't think so.
I haven't got it.	I wouldn't trust him.
He can't swim yet.	They couldn't sleep.
Shouldn't we go?	You haven't eaten.
We didn't sing well.	Math wasn't too hard.
She'll be careful.	They'll come soon.

The WINDMILL is moved BY its surroundings,

but the ELECTRIC FAN MOVES its surroundings.

WHICH ARE YOU?

SILENT LETTERS: "-LE"

We have had a few silent letters so far, like the magic "e" and "-ould." Here are some more. All of these words end with an "l" sound, but are actually spelled "-le." Note that the short-vowel words have double consonants before the "-le" ending. Remember why? See page 83. ("-ckle" words are divided to show spelling pattern only -- they are not usually divided in this way.) Read down each group:

-ckle

ti-ckle
pi-ckle
ca-ckle
cra-ckle

-ple

sim-ple
sam-ple
dim-ple
pim-ple
top-ple
ap-ple

-fle

raf-fle
ruf-fle
muf-fle
shuf-fle

-gle

an-gle
tan-gle
bun-gle
jun-gle
jan-gle
jin-gle
tin-gle
sin-gle

-dle

sad-dle
pad-dle
han-dle
can-dle
mid-dle
mud-dle
noo-dle
poo-dle

-ble

gob-ble
hob-ble
bab-ble
dab-ble
bum-ble
rum-ble
tum-ble
crum-ble
grum-ble
a-ble
ta-ble
ca-ble
fee-ble
bub-ble
dou-ble
trou-ble
ter-ri-ble
hor-ri-ble

-tle

tat-tle
cat-tle
lit-tle
brit-tle
ket-tle

-zle

siz-zle
fiz-zle
raz-zle
daz-zle
nuz-zle
puz-zle
guz-zle

The LESS you talk, the MORE you are listened to!

"-LE" REVIEW

razzle dazzle tickle pickle huddle cuddle
apple dapple cattle tattle simple dimple
feeble steeple jingle jangle middle riddle
sizzle fizzle poodle noodle double trouble
snuffle truffle muddle puddle mumble grumble

shuffle table gobble apple
kettle jingle cattle hobble
double ruffle tickle poodle
sample puzzle jungle puddle
ter-ri-ble trouble hor-ri-ble rumble

tickle cuddle — Gus likes to tickle and cuddle his simple little poodle.

middle muddle — I'm in the middle of a muddle as I fumble with this puzzle!

snuffles truffles — Gus snuffles truffles and his poodle nibbles noodles.

kettle sizzles — The little kettle sizzles, fizzles, and bubbles on the table.

NO dream comes true until you WAKE UP and GO TO WORK!!!

SILENT LETTERS: "K, W, L, M, T, H, GH"

These silent letters are more complicated. This section also may be more difficult because the vowel sounds are quite varied. Therefore, some of the more difficult words are written with diacritical marks for those of you who might find it helpful. HOWEVER -- if it's more confusing than helpful, just cover them up!

k

Read across the page:

knot	knob	knelt
knit	knit-ted	knit-ting
knock	knack	knuck-le
knife	know	known
knee	kneel	kneel-ing

w

wrist	wrap	wreck
wring	wrong	wrung
write	wreath	wrote

l

talk (tôk)	walk (wôk)	stalk (stôk)
half (hăf)	calf (kăf)	chalk (chôk)

knock wrist	knee kneel	stalk calf
wrong knee	knock chalk	write half
half wrong	walk calf	calf kneel
wrap knife	knelt wreck	know walk
knitted wrap	know knack	wrong knob
wring knuckle	knitted wreath	known knot

b

dumb	numb	crumb
lamb	limb	bomb
thumb	thumb-ing	plumb-er
comb	climb	climb-ing

t

of-ten (ôfən)	sof-ten (sôfən)	lis-ten (lĭsən)
nes-tle (nĕsəl)	wres-tle (rĕsəl)	wres-tling
lis-ten-ing	glis-ten (glĭsən)	cas-tle (kăsəl)
has-ten (hāsən)	chas-ten (chāsən)	wres-tling

h

hour (our)	hour-ly	ghet-to (gĕtō)
honest (ŏnĭst)	hon-est-ly	hon-or (ŏnər)
ghost (gōst)	ghast-ly (găstlē)	ghoul (go͞ol)

listen often	castle nestle	climb limb
lamb glisten	ghastly climb	listen ghetto
wrestle crumb	listen whistle	lamb nestle
often wrestle	numb thumb	hourly climb
soften thumb	climbing limb	honest honor
plumber hasten	dumb plumber	ghastly bomb

"SILENT K, W, L, B, T, H" REVIEW

dumb lamb	The dumb lamb knows how to climb in my lap and nestle.
often talk	They often talk and whistle as they hasten up the peaks.
thumb knife	Gus cut his thumb with a knife when he ate half of the calf.
plumber knows	The plumber knows our sink well. Honestly, it is a wreck!
walk castle	We often walk to the castle and listen to the hourly talk.
kneels knocks	She kneels, and knocks half of the knitting from her wrist.
knows knees	She knows how to walk on her knees and her thumbs.
honestly wrong	Honestly, this is the wrong walk. We must hasten home.

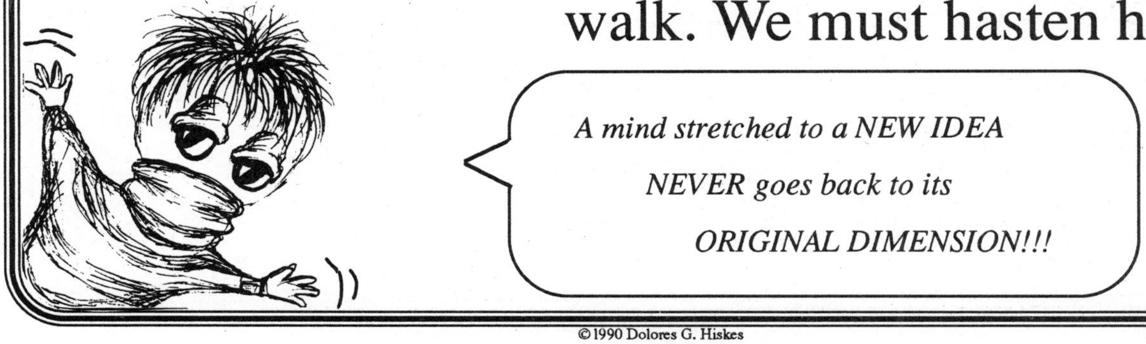
A mind stretched to a NEW IDEA
NEVER goes back to its
ORIGINAL DIMENSION!!!

SILENT "GH"

There are THREE main patterns to silent "gh" -- "igh," "ough," and "augh." (Remember to put a piece of paper underneath the line you are reading if it makes it easier for you, or even try moving your finger underneath each word.) Read across the page:

igh = $\bar{i}$

sigh	sight	slight
fight	flight	fright
tight	right	might
light	slight	bright
night	high	thigh

light sky	tight dive	my thigh
might fly	right flight	might fight
right thigh	night light	slight sigh
light night	high flight	right sight
slight fight	bright light	high flight
fright sight	night flight	thigh high

EACH of us is born with TWO ENDS . . .

ONE to SIT ON,

and ONE to THINK WITH.

SUCCESS depends upon WHICH ONE we use the MOST.

HEADS WE WIN . . . TAILS WE LOSE!!!

ough=ô

ought fought bought
thought sought brought

augh=ô

caught taught daugh-ter
slaugh-ter caught taught

SOME PEOPLE are a LOT LIKE BOATS . . .
They TOOT LOUDEST when they're IN A FOG!!!

sought daughter
fought cause
thought always
brought salt
halt slaughter
bought sauce
crawl caught
brought ball

taught Paul
caught paw
small daughter
bald Maude
Paul ought
almost thought
taught hawk
brought halter

"IGH=Ī," "OUGH, AUGH=Ô" REVIEW

might night	Gus might take a night flight, but he must fight his fright.
brought right	Paul brought the right trick. He thought it might be taught.
ought thought	She ought to have thought of her bright daughter.
daughter might	His daughter might put bright lights on her high tree.
fought night	The thief fought in the night but got caught in the light.
sighed thought	I sighed as I thought of how I sought for the right dog.
fight fright-ful	The fight was a frightful sight, and was brought to a halt.

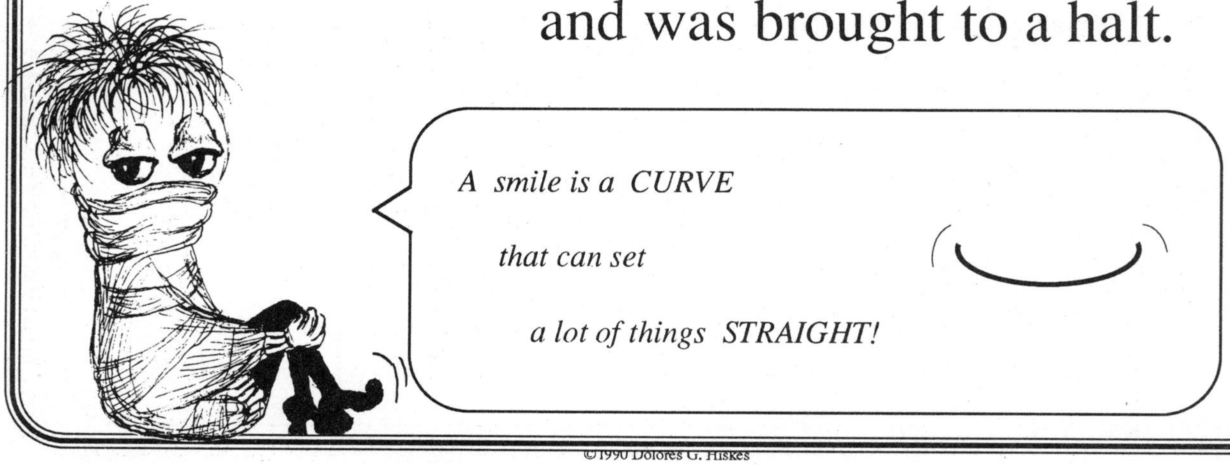
A smile is a CURVE
that can set
a lot of things STRAIGHT!

LONG "A" SPELLING PATTERNS

Sometimes "ei" and "eigh" sound like long "a:"

ei=ā

vein	veil	skein
feign (silent "g")	rein	rein-deer

eigh=ā

Here is a new verse to the poem we learned on page 139. Read across the page:

"'I' before 'e' except after 'c,'
or when sounding like 'a'
as in 'neighbor' or 'weigh!'"

eight	eighth	sleigh
weigh	weight	freight
neigh	neigh-ing	weigh-ing
neigh-bor	neigh-bor-ly	neigh-bor-hood

Keep yourself CLEAN and BRIGHT . . .
YOU are the WINDOW through which
you must SEE THE WORLD!

eight veils	neighbor	weigh sleigh
weigh freight	eighth sleigh	weigh skein
vein weight	weigh veil	eight sleighs
reindeer neigh	feign vein	neighborhood

There are two more spelling patterns for long "a:"

ey=ā

they	prey	o-bey
hey	sur-vey	grey

ea=ā

steak	break	great
rump-steak	break-in	great-ness

"EI, EIGH, EY, EA=Ā" REVIEW

they weigh	grey sleigh	they prey
neighborly	eighth break	obey survey
great veil	they obey	hey freight
sleigh rein	break survey	steak neigh
great steak	make sleigh	ate rumpsteak
they weigh	veil great	hey obey

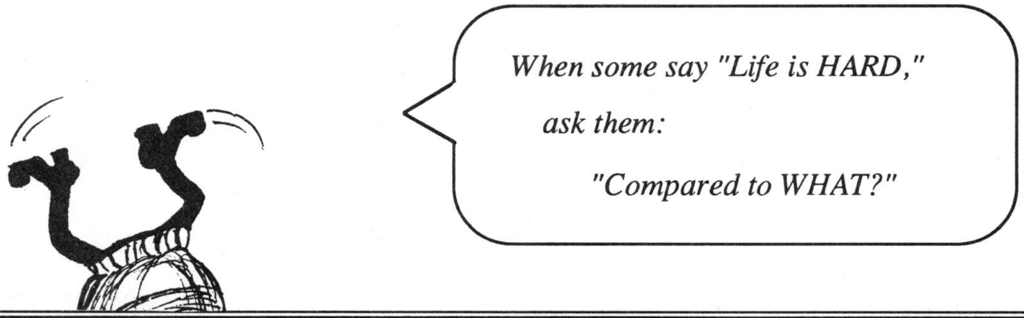

When some say "Life is HARD,"
ask them:
"Compared to WHAT?"

"EI, EIGH, EY, EA=Ā" REVIEW

obeyed eighth	They obeyed, and grabbed the eighth rein on the sleigh.
they survey	They survey their prey and think, "Great rumpsteak!"
neighborhood	They wore their great veils in the gray neighborhood.
eight gained	Gus ate eight great steaks, and he gained a lot of weight.
great break	They pray the great doctor will not break eight veins.
they sleigh	They played on a great sleigh pulled by eight tiny reindeer.
neighbors	Eight great neighbors stay to help weigh the freight.

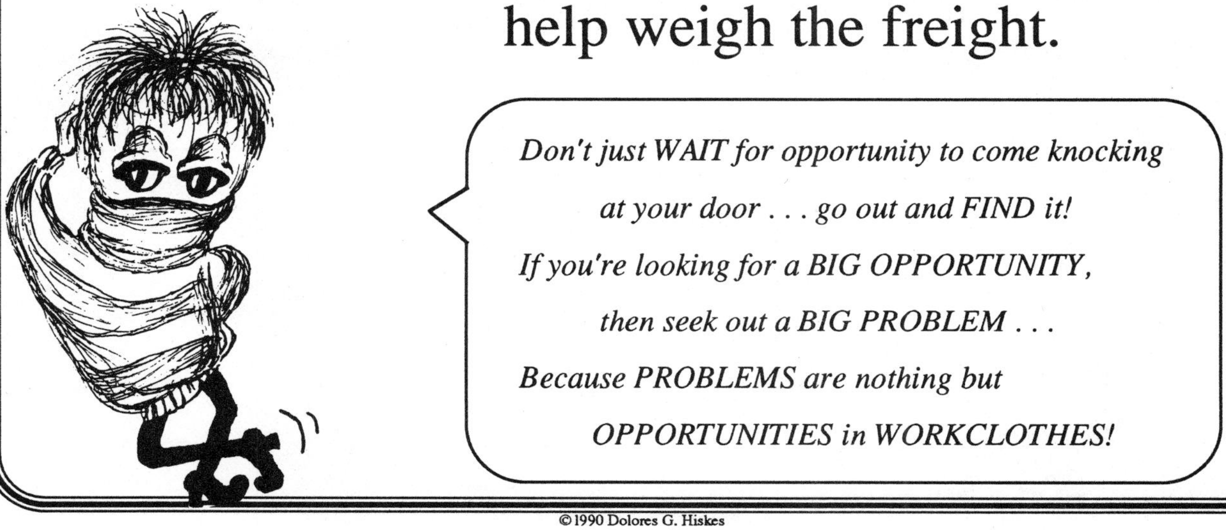

Don't just WAIT for opportunity to come knocking at your door . . . go out and FIND it!
If you're looking for a BIG OPPORTUNITY, then seek out a BIG PROBLEM . . .
Because PROBLEMS are nothing but OPPORTUNITIES in WORKCLOTHES!

"S=Z, PH & GH=F, CH=K"

se=z

On page 40 we learned four words where "s" sounds like "z" -- is, his, as, and has. Here are some more. Read across the page:

rose	pose	nose
rise	a-rise	wise
ease	tease	please
chose	choose	cheese
use	fuse	re-fuse
pause	clause	be-cause

A few words have an "sh" or "sz" sound: sure

plea-sure mea-sure trea-sure

choose treasure	sure please
tease because	use nose
chose pause	wise Rose
measure clause	cause pleasure
please rise	tease Rose
pause because	refuse cheese

The real voyage of discovery consists

not in seeking NEW LANDSCAPES,

but in having NEW EYES!

"S=Z" REVIEW

pleased treasure	I am pleased beyond measure to win that great treasure.
surely measure	It's surely not easy to measure the alligator's long nose.
pleasure because	Gus gets pleasure because his nose is in the cheese.
pauses refuses	Rose pauses, and wisely refuses to choose the easy path.
chose because	She chose to pause because the rose bush was thorny.
refused teasing	He was sad because she refused to stop teasing Rose.
pauses nose	He pauses to blow his nose because he has a cold.

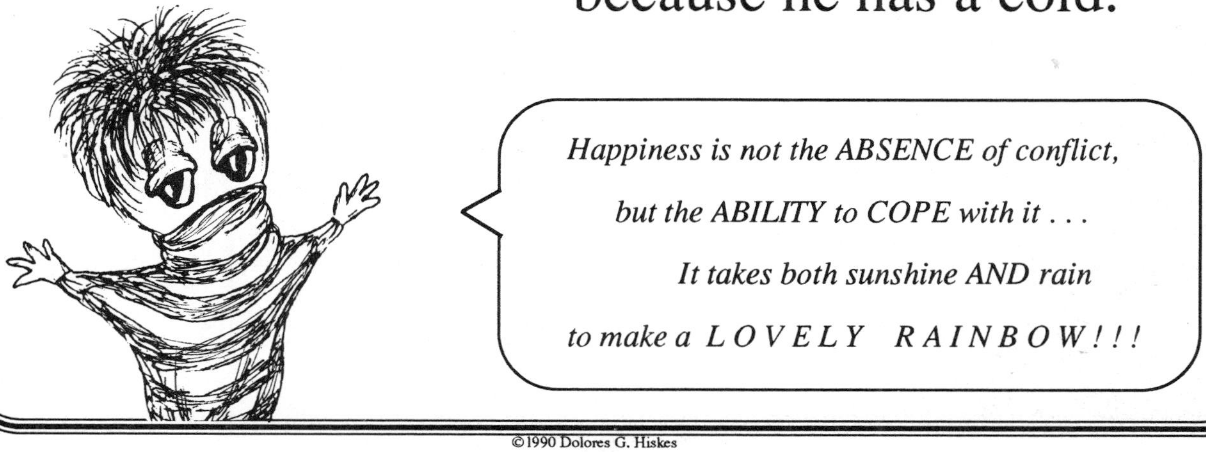
Happiness is not the ABSENCE of conflict,
but the ABILITY to COPE with it . . .
It takes both sunshine AND rain
to make a L O V E L Y   R A I N B O W ! ! !

ph=f

Read across the page:

phone	pho-ny	tel-e-phone
phon-ics	or-phan	pho-to-graph
phase	phrase	pho-no-graph
phys-ics	phys-i-cal	Phil-ip
pam-phlet	el-e-phant	phan-tom

phony phantom	elephant photo
telephone orphan	orphan elephant
physics pamphlet	physical phase
phantom photograph	phonics phrase
Philip's phonograph	Phil's telephone

gh=f

Read across the page:

rough (rŭf)	e-nough (enŭf)	tough (tŭf)
laugh (lâf)	laugh-ing	cough (kôf)

FREEDOM begins BETWEEN YOUR EARS!!!

tough cough	laugh enough
rough laugh	enough coughing
enough laughing	tough enough

"PH, GH=F" REVIEW

(Read across the page)

Philip laugh	Philip photograph
telephone Phil	phony telephone
enough phonics	enough laughter
elephant cough	rough cough
laughing orphan	laughing elephant
tough physical	tough phrase

laugh phantom	They laugh and laugh at the phony phantom.
'phone rough	'Phone Phil -- he has a rough cough and is in bed.
elephant tough	Be careful! That elephant is tough and rough.
orphan enough	That orphan has had enough rough times. Let's help!
photograph Phil	Photograph Phil and his fancy physics pamphlet.
Phil phonics	Both Phil and Gus have had enough phonics today.

When you CAN'T CHANGE the DIRECTION of the WIND -- ADJUST YOUR SAILS!!!

ch=k

Read across the page:

Chris-tie	chris-ten	Christ-mas
school	schol-ar	schol-as-tic
chord	chor-us	ache
chron-ic	chron-i-cle	chem-ist
scheme	sched-ule	Chris-to-pher

christen Chris	school chronicle
chronic chord	chemist scheme
Christmas chorus	Christie scholar
Christopher ache	scholastic schedule

schedule Christie — Shall we schedule a day to christen baby Christie?

chemist scheme — The chemist has a scheme that will cure a chronic cough.

Christopher aches — Christopher aches to sing in the Christmas chorus.

school schedule — Chris has a very long school schedule this year.

Never let what you CAN'T do

interfere with what you CAN do!

ANOTHER "R" MODIFIED VOWEL SOUND
ÂR=-AIR, -ARE, -EAR, -ERE"

When we add an "e" to a word ending in "-ar," the sound changes, as well as the meaning. The "MAGIC 'E'" strikes AGAIN! When a word ends in "-are," it usually sounds like "air." There are several ways to spell this sound:

are=âr

fare	care	dare	bare
share	stare	glare	rare
spare	scare	snare	dare
Mar-y	blare	flare	pare

air=âr

air	fair	pair	hair
lair	stair	flair	Claire

ear=âr

bear	tear	wear	pear

ere=âr

where there (means "direction")

ONE MORE word has this sound. It sounds exactly like the word "there," but is SPELLED differently and has a completely different MEANING:

their *(means "belonging to")*

Where are their cakes? Over there?

"ARE, AIR, EAR=ÂR" REVIEW

scare bear	dare Mary	rare pear
Claire wear	where chair	snare lair
share chair	bear stare	stair there
rare pair	share fare	fair Claire
their share	spare bear	wear pair

share chair — Mary, please share that fair chair over there with Claire.

where hairy — Where is the rare pair of black hairy bears?

stare tear — They stare at the tear there in my spare pair of pants.

pair bears — The pair of bears glares and stares in their lair under the stairs.

Claire pears — Mary and Claire both ate their fair share of rare pears.

dares wear — Mary dares Gus to wear his rare pair of boots to the fair.

The GREATEST OAK was once a LITTLE NUT that HELD ITS GROUND!!!

A SPELLING GRAB BAG

This section deals with some spelling rules which are really useful to know. (They are not necessary to know in order to read, however, and you may wish to just read them for now, and learn these rules more thoroughly at a later date.)

Homonyms

Strictly speaking, true homonyms have the same sound and spelling, but different meanings. The meaning needed is determined by the context of the word within the sentence:

I **can** read well. We **can** apples in the Fall.

I cannot **bear** snakes. He saw big **bear** tracks.

That **rose** is very red. I **rose** from my chair.

Homophones

On page 185 we learned about two words that sound exactly the same, as homonyms do, but have different *spellings* as well as meanings -- "their and there." These kind of words are called HOMOPHONES. Homophones certainly make life complicated when it comes to spelling! The more you read, however, the better able you will be to select the correct spelling when you need to write any of these words.

Write a simple sentence using each of the words listed below. Use the dictionary to find out the meaning of any word you're not sure of:

here hear
do due
shoe shoo
break brake
no know
shone shown
raise rays
cheep cheap

to two too
blue blew
pane pain
steak stake
great grate
there their
steel steal
choose chews

If you CAN"T get people to LISTEN ANY OTHER WAY, tell them it's a SECRET!!!

(SSSSSSsshhhhhhh....)

There are many more. I'll bet YOU can think of some I haven't listed here! (It's fun to keep a list, and see how many you can come up with.)

Homographs

HOMOGRAPHS, like homonyms, are words which are spelled the same way and have different meanings. But homographs usually have different *pronunciations* as well! As with homonyms, it's easy to tell which particular meaning we need, just by reading the sentence. This "context clue" will tell us exactly which word fits.

Ben likes to **read** books.
Ben **read** a book today.

Nobody ever left FOOTPRINTS in the SANDS OF TIME BY SITTING DOWN!!!

The actor took a **bow** at the end of the play.
Katie had a big, fat, pink **bow** in her hair.

Gus got a big **tear** in his pants.
She felt sad, and a **tear** rolled down her cheek.

We **live** in a small, wooden house.
I like to hear a **live** band best of all!

The **dove** sang and sang in the big oak tree.
Jan **dove** in the water, but bumped her head.

Gus will **lead** us to the table with cream cakes.
Gus' tummy feels as heavy as a lump of **lead**.

HOMONYMS: Words that have the *same sound and spelling,* but different *meanings.*
HOMOPHONES: Words that have the *same sound only,* but usually different *spellings* (as well as meanings).
HOMOGRAPHS: Words that have the *same spelling only,* but usually different *sounds* (as well as meanings).

Multi-syllable word endings

On page 83 we learned that when we add endings to short-vowel words finishing with only one consonant we must first double that consonant before adding the ending. Those words all had one syllable. In a multi-syllable word, if the accent is on the LAST short-vowel syllable, we STILL need to double that last consonant before adding an ending:

sub-mit	sub-mit-ted	sub-mit-ting
ad-mit	ad-mit-ted	ad-mit-ting
per-mit	per-mit-ted	per-mit-ting
com-pel	com-pel-led	com-pel-ling

If the accent is NOT on the last syllable, we do NOT double the final consonant before adding endings, in order to keep the short-vowel sound:

mar-ket	mar-ket-ed	mar-ket-ing
vis-it	vis-it-ed	vis-it-ing
trum-pet	trum-pet-ed	trum-pet-ing
hap-pen	hap-pen-ed	hap-pen-ing

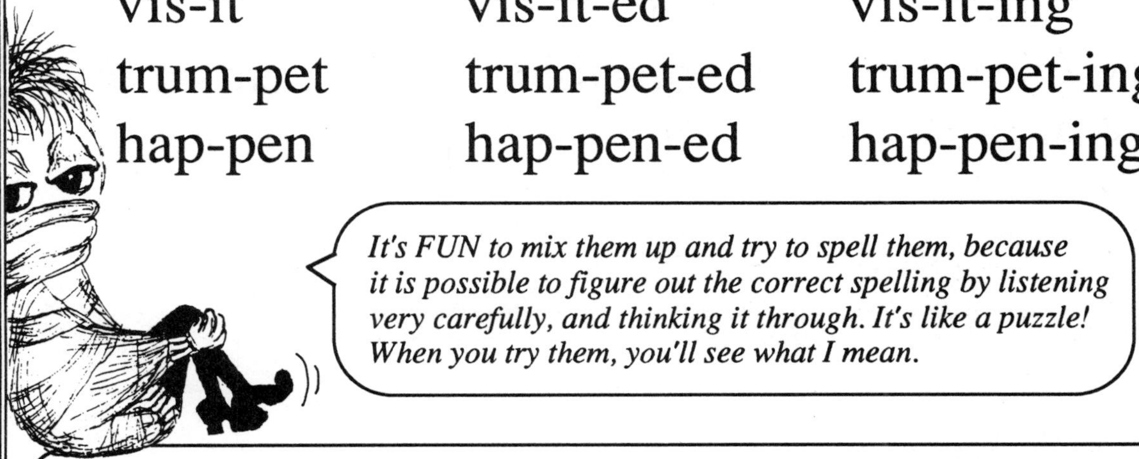
It's FUN to mix them up and try to spell them, because it is possible to figure out the correct spelling by listening very carefully, and thinking it through. It's like a puzzle! When you try them, you'll see what I mean.

admitted	visited	permitted
submitting	trumpeting	visiting
happened	compelled	marketed
permitting	happening	admitting
submitted	trumpeted	visited

"-ce, -ge" plus endings

When a word ends in "-ce" or "-ge," we KEEP the "e" before adding"-ous" or "-able." This is done to keep the "j" sound of "g" and the "s" sound of "c:"

out-ra-geous	gor-geous	cou-ra-geous
peace-able	change-able	trace-able
no-tice-able	re-place-able	dam-age-able

"-able, -ible"

If a word is complete in itself WITHOUT the ending, we usually use "-able." If not -- most of the time (but not always!) we spell it "-ible:"

read-able	tax-able	pre-fer-able
suit-able	rea-son-able	pre-vent-able
cred-ible	vis-ible	ed-ible
pos-sible	ter-rible	com-pat-ible

People are like stained glass windows . . .
They SPARKLE and SHINE
when the SUN is out,
but when the DARKNESS sets in
their TRUE BEAUTY is revealed
ONLY if there is a L I G H T W I T H I N!

PREFIXES: "PRE-, SUB-, RE-, AUTO-"

A PREFIX is a syllable that is attached to the front of a word. Usually this changes its meaning. There are many prefixes, but we shall try just a few, so that you can see what they are.

pre- (means before, or in front of)

pre-mix	pre-cool	pre-heat
pre-judge	pre-ma-ture	pre-pay

sub- (means under, or beneath)

sub-way	sub-let	sub-ma-rine
sub-di-vide	sub-mit	sub-tract
sub-con-tract	sub-arc-tic	sub-merge

re- (usually means again, back)

re-act	re-do	re-copy
re-cov-er	re-place	re-paint
re-heat	re-fresh	re-turn

auto- (means by oneself, or itself)

auto-mat	auto-mo-bile	auto-bus
auto-mat-ic	auto-mo-tive	auto-graph

A DWARF standing on the shoulders of a GIANT can sometimes SEE FARTHER than the GIANT HIMSELF!

"UN-, DIS-, INTER-, SUPER-"

un- (means the reverse of)

un-zip
un-seen
un-kind
un-able
un-like
un-cov-er
un-done
un-hap-py
un-luck-y

dis- (means the reverse of)

dis-able
dis-a-gree
dis-col-or
dis-pose
dis-o-bey
dis-cov-er

inter- (means between two things)

inter-act
inter-change
inter-lock
inter-mix
inter-com
inter-view

super- (means extra, or above)

super-mom
super-son-ic
super-vi-sor
super-hu-man
super-in-tend-ent
super-sen-si-tive
super-heat
super-vise
super-pow-er
super-mar-ket
super-im-pose
super-no-va

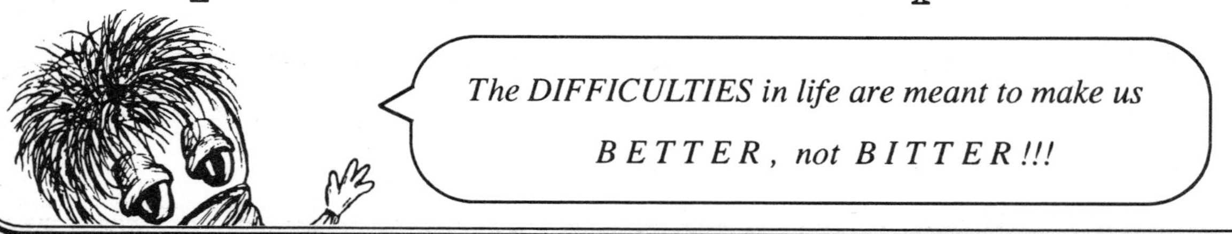

The DIFFICULTIES in life are meant to make us
BETTER, not BITTER!!!

PREFIX REVIEW

re-dis-cov-er super-no-va
rediscover supernova

inter-view super-mom
interview supermom

un-hap-py super-vi-sor
unhappy supervisor

inter-view super-pow-er
interview superpower

sub-merge sub-ma-rine
submerge submarine

pre-judge super-in-ten-dent
prejudge superintendent

sub-arc-tic super-mar-ket
subarctic supermarket

super-sen-si-tive auto-mo-bile
supersensitive automobile

The BEST and most BEAUTIFUL things in the WORLD CANNOT be SEEN, nor TOUCHED. . . but are FELT IN THE H E A R T.

SUFFIXES: "-TION,-SION,-ABLE,-NESS,-FUL,-LESS,-MENT"

A SUFFIX is a syllable that is added at the end of a word. There are many -- we shall try just a few. (The "-tion" or "-sion" suffix sounds like "shun.")

-tion

sta-tion	ad-di-tion
na-tion	ad-dic-tion
por-tion	ac-tion
va-ca-tion	in-vi-ta-tion
pro-mo-tion	at-ten-tion
ed-u-ca-tion	foun-da-tion
sec-tion	af-fec-tion

-sion

mis-sion
im-pres-sion
ex-pres-sion
ex-plo-sion
ex-ten-sion
vi-sion
tel-e-vi-sion

-able

lov-able	pass-able	print-able
dur-able	en-able	dis-able
like-able	port-able	prob-able
de-sir-able	ca-pable	no-table
pre-sent-able	con-sid-er-able	im-prob-able
in-com-par-able	in-dis-pen-sable	val-u-able
in-es-cap-able	for-mid-able	de-lec-table
a-dor-able	per-ish-able	in-ca-pable

When you were BORN, you CRIED and the world REJOICED.
Live your life in such a way that when you DIE,
the WORLD cries, and YOU rejoice!!!

-ness

good-ness	thick-ness	dark-ness
kind-ness	weak-ness	ill-ness
mad-ness	soft-ness	well-ness
nice-ness	bad-ness	wil-der-ness

-ful (means full of)

play-ful	hope-ful	fear-ful
faith-ful	care-ful	pain-ful
for-get-ful	harm-ful	use-ful
won-der-ful	for-get-ful	thank-ful

-less (means without)

rest-less	reck-less	need-less
shift-less	help-less	end-less
worth-less	price-less	time-less
hope-less	point-less	worth-less

-ment

place-ment	move-ment	treat-ment
state-ment	base-ment	a-bate-ment
pun-ish-ment	re-place-ment	re-fresh-ment
pave-ment	en-gage-ment	gov-ern-ment

WHO is right is NEVER so important as WHAT is right!!!

SUFFIX REVIEW

won-der-ful in-vi-ta-tion
wonderful invitation

pre-sent-able gov-ern-ment
presentable government

in-com-par-able va-ca-tion
incomparable vacation

in-dis-pen-sable foun-da-tion
indispensable foundation

for-mid-able mis-sion
formidable mission

de-sir-able pro-mo-tion
desirable promotion

lov-able ex-pres-sion
lovable expression

price-less wil-der-ness
priceless wilderness

The WORST PRISON OF ALL is the one INSIDE of a CLOSED HEART!!!

COMPOUND WORDS

A COMPOUND WORD is made by joining two complete words together to make a new word. It's fun to read the words listed below and determine which two words each one is made of!

anything	hillside	understand
classroom	without	bedroom
somebody	freeway	downtown
paycheck	clipboard	homework
playground	brainwash	earthquake
outdoors	supermarket	workout
datebook	overcome	pathways
superman	buckskin	footbridge
daybreak	hunchback	something
crackdown	tablecloth	underworld
superpower	underground	footsteps

May we have the PEACE and SERENITY to accept the things we CANNOT CHANGE,

. . . the COURAGE to change the things we CAN,

. . . and the WISDOM TO KNOW THE DIFFERENCE!!!

"BUILDING BLOCKS"

In each group of words, the top word is a part of every word listed below it. You will be building WORDS from blocks of SYLLABLES. Try it -- it's fun!

board
board-ing
key-board
clip-board

check
check-er
re-check
pay-check

rage
en-rage
en-rag-ing
out-ra-geous

pass
under-pass
sur-pass-ing
un-sur-pass-able

back
back-ing
back-ward
out-back

front
front-ward
con-front
con-fron-ta-tion

press
ex-press
in-ex-press-i-ble
com-press-ing

cover
un-cover
un-re-cover-able
dis-cover-ing

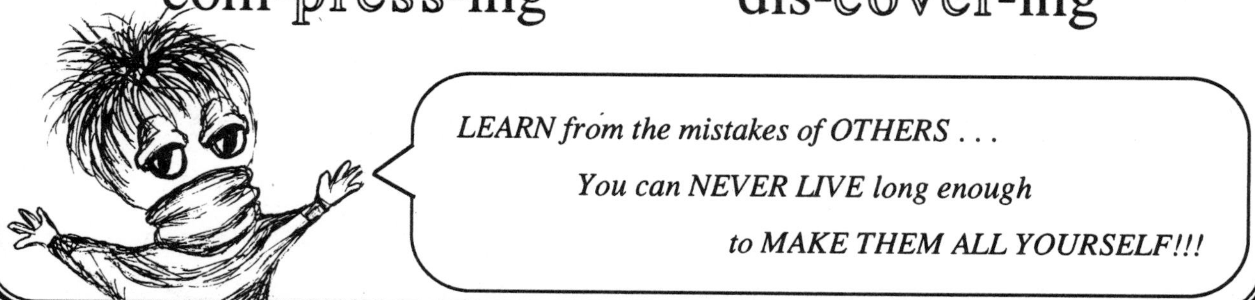
LEARN from the mistakes of OTHERS . . .
You can NEVER LIVE long enough
to MAKE THEM ALL YOURSELF!!!

mark
re-mark
re-mark-able
un-re-mark-able

come
wel-come
wel-com-ing
over-com-ing

see
fore-see
fore-see-able
un-fore-see-able

fort
com-fort
ef-fort
fort-ress
ef-fort-less
com-fort-able
com-fort-ing-ly

quake
Quak-er
quak-ing
earth-quake

force
en-force
force-ful-ness
re-in-force-ment

give
for-give
for-giv-able
un-for-giv-able

agree
agree-able
agree-ment
agree-ing
dis-agree
dis-agree-able
dis-agree-ment

WINNERS NEVER QUIT, and QUITTERS NEVER WIN!!!

tend
in-tend
in-tend-ing
super-in-tend-ent

under
under-stand
mis-under-stand
mis-under-stand-ing

mark
mar-ket
mar-ket-ing
mar-ket-able
mar-ket-a-bil-i-ty

sent
pre-sent
pre-sent-ed
pre-sent-able
un-pre-sent-able

tract
sub-tract
sub-tract-able
un-sub-tract-able

light
light-en
light-en-ing
de-light-ful

pen
play-pen
pen-cil
in-dis-pen-sa-ble
car-pen-ter

press
im-press
im-pres-sion
im-pres-sion-able
im-pres-sion-is-tic

FRIENDSHIP is like a BEAUTIFUL GARDEN . . .
The MORE you put INTO it, the BETTER it GROWS!!!

way
way-side
side-ways

mark
re-mark
re-mark-able
un-re-mark-able

new
re-new
new-ness
un-re-new-able

wild
wild-fire
wil-der-ness

sense
non-sense
non-sen-si-cal
sen-si-tive
super-sen-si-tive

nap
nap-kin
kid-nap

land
land-mark
play-land
out-land-ish-ly

pass
pass-able
sur-pass
un-sur-pass-able

cord
re-cord-ing
dis-cord-ant

port
im-port
im-por-tant
trans-port
trans-por-ta-tion

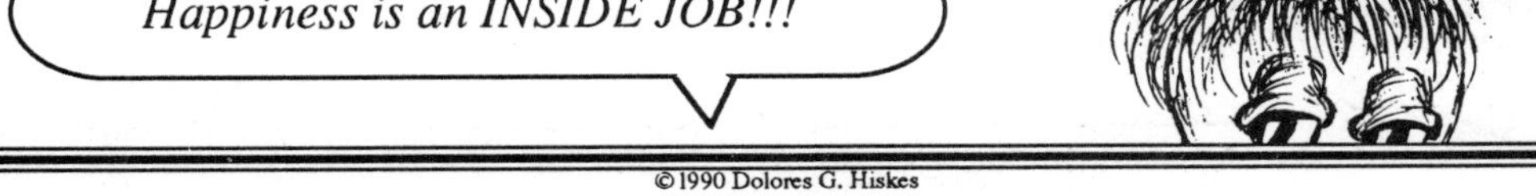

His won-der-ful, re-mark-able auto-mo-bile
has a super-sen-si-tive inter-com.

A super-no-va is a fan-tas-tic star that can
sud-den-ly shine a bil-lion times bright-er!

He seems to have a hope-less ad-dic-tion to
worth-less tel-e-vi-sion pro-grams.

She went to con-sid-er-able length to be help-ful
af-ter that dev-as-tat-ing earth-quake.

I have the im-pres-sion that Gus loves end-less
por-tions of de-lec-table re-fresh-ments.

It is im-prob-able that we will dis-cov-er any
more gold in that hill-side wil-der-ness.

Aus-tra-lia has out-land-ish-ly huge croc-o-diles
in its re-mark-able out-back.

Life ITSELF can't give you joy,
Unless you really WILL it . . .
Life just gives you TIME and SPACE,
It's up to YOU to FILL IT!!!

Supermom's performance went fantastically well.

It is time to submerge the submarine. NOW!

I'm cold! This must be a subarctic supermarket.

Gus thinks he is going on a formidable mission.

Her cats possess the most lovable expressions.

Soon she is going on an incomparable vacation.

Phonics is an unsurpassable tool for reading.

His expression at that moment was unprintable.

A strong foundation to a house is indispensable.

. . . And now, my in-es-cap-able, un-a-void-able im-pres-sion is that we have just fin-ished this con-sid-er-able, re-mark-able, fan-tas-ti-cal-ly won-der-ful book . . . . . . this is THE END!!

We are all travelers as we pass over
the hills and valleys of life . . .
But the journey of a thousand miles
STILL begins with
JUST
ONE
STEP . . .
As did your journey through Phonics Pathways.
So where will you GO now, and what will you DO?
It's a choice that's entirely UP TO YOU!
But WHEREVER you go and WHATEVER you do . . .

"THIS ABOVE ALL . . .
TO THINE OWN SELF BE TRUE."

--William Shakespeare

Thank you for letting my work become part of your lives.

Dolores

ABOUT THE AUTHOR

Dolores G. Hiskes has been involved with education most of her adult life. Throughout the years she has written and produced a variety of community programs for young people, as well as several newsletters and many newspaper articles. She co-authored a work-study manual for the local high school, and edited several books for its English classes. While working at Las Positas College she developed an original filing system for the Career Center and gave seminars to other career center personnel on how to set up and use that system. She also gave workshops to Las Positas students on résumé building and interview techniques, and introductory programs to new students on college rules, regulations and graduation requirements. Painting and writing remain on-going hobbies.

Literacy, however, has remained her life-long passion, ever since her own children first needed help in learning how to read. She taught them using a phonics-based teaching method she created, and has developed and refined this technique while tutoring others for almost thirty years. Throughout her years of travel she has studied innumerable old mostly-out-of-print textbooks from all over the world. She gradually conceived of a way to simplify and better organize this expanding body of information, incorporating the best of these hard-to-find rules into an up-to-date and easy-to-use book. *Phonics Pathways* is the result of that effort.

Currently, she gives programs and workshops on *Reading: Why We Can't And How We Can,* consults with schools and organizations on setting up in-school and after-school tutoring programs, and continues to write new material. Professional memberships include the Orton Dyslexia Society, LDA (Learning Disabilities Association), CARS (California Association of Resource Specialists), California Lawyers for the Arts, Bookbuilders West, Chicago Book Clinic, Marin Self-Publishers Association, PMA (Publishers Marketing Association), Commonwealth Club of California, and Eastbay Watercolor Society.

Dolores and her husband John live in the Bay Area with Kiwi, a precocious puss who fetches and watches television. They have two grown children -- Robin was a French major who also studied electrical engineering, and today is employed as a systems engineer project manager. After working for years as an emergency rescue climber in Yosemite and on ski patrol at Mammoth, Grant became a paramedic, and is currently back in school full time majoring in biological science.

VISION AND MOTOR COORDINATION TRAINING EXERCISES*

Not all children will be able to do all of these exercises. Try working through them, and see if you can come up with a small group of them that you both enjoy. It is important to practice the ones you have chosen on a regular basis, but you can vary them if you feel a change is needed:

1. Have him hold his head still, and follow with his eyes as you slowly move a small object (penny, head of pencil, etc.) from far left to far right at eye level, back and forth several times. Then move it up and down, and after that diagonally. Always move it slowly and smoothly.

2. Make a beanbag about 5" square (Bird seed makes wonderful filling!) and throw it back and forth to him. (Beanbags are easy to catch and don't roll away when dropped.) Aim for a faster throw and catch. (He may wish to change to a ball when this skill is well-developed.)

3. Have him lie on the ground, and tell him to raise his left leg, right leg, left arm, or right arm. When he can do each of them easily, then say two together -- "Left leg, right arm," "right leg, right arm," etc.

4. While he is on the ground, tell him to make "angels in the snow" -- to move his arms and legs up and down against the ground. Then say a particular arm or leg, as in above exercise. When he gets proficient, have him combine an arm with a leg upon command, as above.

5. Have him walk on a balance board (holding his hands if necessary), or some variation of it. He can even walk on a rope laid across the floor, one foot in front of the other, all along the rope.

6. Have him march to an even beat while you clap or beat a drum, throwing opposite arms and legs forward. Then have him clap and march together.

7. See if he can crawl. If he cannot, have him practice crawling.

8. If a trampoline is available, have him jump on a trampoline. Hold his hand for safety!

9. If he is well-coordinated, have him practice skipping.

(*No special claims for these exercises are made, other than that they were helpful to the author's own children. They may or may not be helpful to others. Check with your doctor before proceeding.)

10. Have him make large, simultaneous circles (chalk on blackboard or fingers on wall) with both hands at the same time. Then reverse direction. Now have him cross hands over, and repeat. (This may be difficult for some children.)

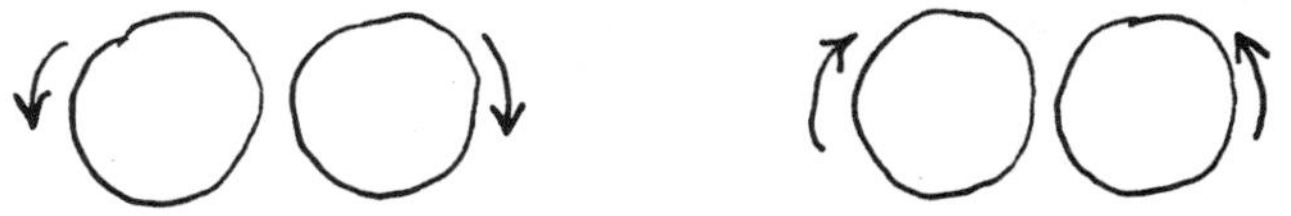

11. If his writing is poor, have him practice the following things with a pencil and paper, working from left to right:

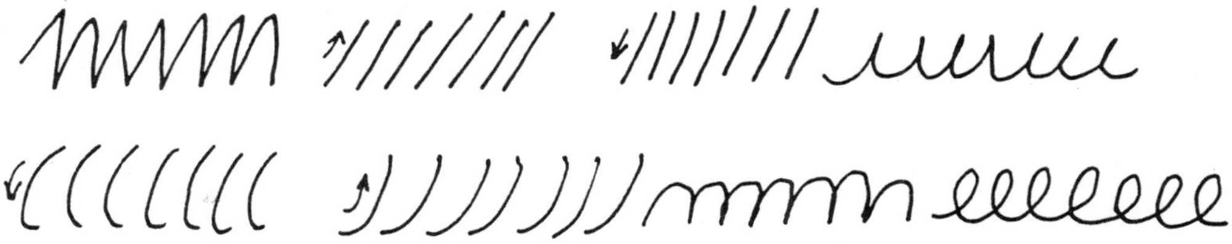

12. Get tracing paper, and have him trace some of his favorite pictures with a pencil. Then have him trace large letters, beginning at the correct spot and moving his pencil in the right direction.

13. Cut out (or buy from a store or catalogue) large, 3" to 6" letters. Sandpaper letters greatly increase this tactile experience! Have him feel each letter with his hands, and then trace it with his fingertip. Always make sure he begins at the correct point and moves in the right direction. (Many little workbooks, or even writing pads, show just how to do this.)

14. To increase the kinesthetic experience, tell him to trace *big* letters with his fingertip on the wall (or chalk on blackboard if available). Always make sure he moves in the right direction.

15. Suspend a whiffle ball (plastic ball with cutouts) from the ceiling or rafter in the garage, about chest level. Have him "box" with alternate fists, aiming for a smooth, even stroke. Then have him hit the ball with a bat, always trying to move it in the same center direction.

16. Suspend this ball at foot level, slightly off the floor. Have him kick with alternate feet, aiming for a smooth, even kick, sending the ball in the same center direction each time. After awhile, as he kicks with his left foot have him move his right arm slightly forward, and his left arm slightly back, alternating arms with legs.

May you always find
NEW ROADS TO TRAVEL . . .
NEW HORIZONS TO EXPLORE . . .
and NEW DREAMS
to CALL
YOUR
OWN!!!